DELIVERANCE IN THE MIDST OF PAIN

Taking Charge Of My Destiny With A New Perspective

SHARMETRA AUBREY LEWIS

bli PUBLISHING

DELIVERANCE IN THE MIDST OF PAIN

Taking Charge Of My Destiny With A New Perspective

SHARMETRA AUBREY LEWIS

Deliverance In The Midst of Pain: Taking Charge of My Destiny With a New Perspective

Produced by BLI Publishing, LLC
P.O. Box 1931
Cedar Hill, TX 75106
USA
469-557-1254 | www.BLIPublishing.com | info@blipublishing.com

Book cover, layout and editing completed by BLI Publishing, LLC. All rights reserved.

Published in the United States of America. Printed via Createspace.

ISBN-13: 978-1-6969814-5-3

ACKNOWLEDGMENTS

To all those who played a vital role in my life, I thank you dearly. To the naysayers and whisperers, my journey has only begun. To my husband Roc, I thank you for your continual patience and understanding and to my loving daughter Tori, I can't wait to see what great writings you go on to complete for yourself. Most importantly, thank you God for this journey, and the courage to share it with others.

Table Of Contents

Fighting For Love   107

Fighting For The Kingdom   137

Introduction

Leaning over the caged, approximately four feet tall, light grey wall, called a cubicle, holding me in contemporary confinement, I whispered, "Hey, sorry to bother, but do you have some Clorox cleaning wipes I can use to clean off my desk?"

Confused, but now certainly distracted, my neighbor laughs, "No, but why do you even want to clean off your desk? I'm sure it wasn't clean when the last person left it?"

As true as that was, for some reason my grandmother's drilled in morals rested upon me and I could hear her sweet southern voice saying, "Whether you're moving in, moving on, or moving out, don't leave your place nasty."

Hot diggity dog, was I excited! I couldn't wait to finish cleaning and packing up, so I could be released from that metaphoric, rabbit trap, and run swiftly after my destiny. Walking around soliciting cleaning products, I felt the tension in the room but despite all the efforts, people portrayed as busyness. Finally getting my hands on some Clorox, Fraganzia, I grabbed a handful of paper towels and went to town cleaning every spot that looked like it belonged to me. With each sprinkle of fresh Island Orchid Clorox particles descending down on my desk, I couldn't help but see why they call it a multipurpose cleaner. It's ironic because with my natural eyes, I saw the Clorox wiping away the accumulated dirt scum, but with my spiritual eyes, I saw the grace of God gracefully cleaning things up and making room for my new beginnings. At last, 9:30 a.m. had arrived. My two-weeks' notice was down to the final minute and there was no longer a future anticipation of leaving my workplace captivity, but a present reality. I began making my rounds towards the entrance that was now my final exit with my small brown box packed, and a banana pudding pan sitting on top of it. I could feel the genuine love in the atmosphere, as everyone hugged me and wished me the best of luck on my new adventure. There wasn't a soul in the office who was shocked when they learned that I was resigning from my position with Thanksgiving and Christmas right around the corner.

Who knows, maybe I'll be the 100th customer again and win a Thanksgiving turkey at the local neighborhood car wash. If Santa Claus was real, then maybe he granted my gift of fearlessness a month and two weeks earlier, because nothing at that point could stop me. Struggling to hold onto my box and delicious banana pudding, my manager quickly grabbed it before it hit the floor. It would've been a going away meal for the office rats and roaches, if any happened to be in the building, that day.

I couldn't leave the building without a plethora of questions: "So, what are you going to do now?" "How are you going to make it?" "Why didn't you wait until the first of the year, like I'm doing?" "Are you scared to leave this good job?" "What about your benefits?" "What if you don't find another job that pays you as much as this one did?"

Every question expressed their own fears of losing what they, themselves saw as job security. Smiling with understanding, I insisted, "I'm stepping out on faith, to do God's will. I have a mission to complete, books to write, and a passion to be fulfill, that can't be fulfilled hiding behind these heavily secured comforting walls."

Squinting their eyes, in both amazement and doubt, I could tell it must have been a while since God has made a believer out of someone else's faith.

Reassuring my sanity, I smiled and said, "I don't know what the future may hold nor what's ahead of me, but what I do know is that God is repositioning me. If I don't move obediently, then I know He'll move me one way or another, and besides, my faith is greater than my fears. I'm no longer afraid to run after my destiny and I'm tired of settling for less, than his promise for me."

"Amen sister," a shout came from the background, before fading back into silence.

Hugging me tightly, my dear friend fought through the tears, "I wish you were my daughter."

One guy, who has never said two words to me said, "I wish I had your courage."

Trying to reflect my courage like a mirror, I whispered back, "Yes you do, I'm sure it's in there somewhere."

Certain that it wasn't he insisted, "No, I'm not courageous, that's why I'm still here.

Now, I always knew that so many people sacrificed their dreams and ambitions for fear of failure, but it was in this moment of showing my courage, that I realized how the lack of courage in the corporate world was seriously a big deal. Finally, reaching my exit to freedom, I looked back one last time with gratitude. I was so grateful for God favoring me enough to grant me an experience of working for a well-knowing, well-paying, growing corporation, but, I was excited to know that this job was just one more completed traveling point along my journey. It was certainly not my stopping point, but yet a pivotal point of life. Regenerated by the sun's beaming rays and a whirling wind gently blowing against my face, my stomach erupted in excitement. There was an explosion down inside of me as I set off on my path towards destiny's calling. Pain had been pushing me all year, forcing me to pay closer attention to the soul felt vision pulling me. Destiny's call was loud and clear. No more could I tune it out, instead, I welcomed it. Words can't begin to even explain that moment of enlightenment.

Now, I know what you're probably thinking, 'Wow! She is crazy courageous!'

Can I tell you the truth? I haven't always been this bold and courageous. In fact, I was just like everyone else, scared and afraid to put my faith in God, above all things. Can we talk about this sad and powerful word FEAR, for a minute?

Fear, as small as this four-letter word is, has the ability and magnitude to destroy and cripple every part of our being, which is simply ludicrous. The mere thought of it makes us run, hide, and tuck our heads underneath what we call safety. Ironically, the more we play it safe, the more we enslave ourselves, hindering our ability to allow God's presence to navigate for us when we cannot navigate for ourselves. If I had to sit before a jury, one month before finishing this book, then I would've been guilty of trying to lead my own life into my unforeseen destiny. I would've been without a doubt... GUILTY AS CHARGED! I would have been convicted of being afraid of trusting God wholeheartedly. I'm not just talking about trusting Him when things work out the way I expected them to, because everything is in alignment with my so-called goals, dreams, and aspirations. I'm speaking particularly about the times when all hell broke loose and life felt like a great big mistake because the actualization of that hell was not in my glamorous composition notebook plan.

I'd have to glance over my list of charges, written in red ink, and see again a charge for losing hope. See instead of living my life full of purpose and passion, I began losing hope that I really could have the life I envisioned. The enemy often attacked and weakened my confidence, and reminded me of my upbringings. I'd hear in my mind things like, "You'll never be wealthy. Your family always had to struggle to make ends meet." Fear would nick pick even more by bragging about the accomplishments of those around me, "Look at everything your friends had growing up, and you couldn't afford it."

Before I could see the blessing in the trials, my siblings and I had to endure; fear and the lack of prosperity had already begun spreading its poison into the deepest parts of my unveiling soul. Whenever I tried pushing forward in my adult life, I found myself looking through the rearview mirror to the years spent seeing my mother struggle, daringly to make ends meet for us. She was a beautiful, hardworking, single mother, of four children, persisting to do the best she could for us. Although helpmates, temporary, place holding, stepdads came and went in the home, we still had to endure the harsh reality of seeing my mom stand firm in who she was, despite having the lights, water, and gas turned off at the most crucial times when we needed it most. One of the homes we grew up in was built by a man who had a vision, my uncle, Lord rest his soul. Appreciative of his craftiness, I am forever grateful, but the home was very frosty, cold during the winter due to large cracks and openings in the structural foundations of the walls and floors. The summers were blistering hot as the air escaped the solitude of our comforting walls. We intentionally kept the front door open and the blinds evenly stretched open as well to display the beautiful and elegant furniture in our home so the neighbors could admire. How exciting! But that temporary excitement quickly drifted into depression when Rent-A-Center took hold of our elegant display time and time again, leaving our living room vacant and sadly empty.

I was reminded how in the late 1990's, we had to utilize areas of our backyard as our personal restroom due to the one toilet in the house that was damaged. When the weather conditions were unsuitable for such business, we had to use a bucket in a room that was off limits to the rest of the house. It's humorous to me now, because I honestly think I could have survived the cave man days with all the challenges I had to overcome. Trust me, these instances are only the beginning of my story.

One particular challenge that my sister and I like to share, as it reminds us to never forget where we came from as if forgetting is something easy to do, happened later in life. I was in high school at the time when it was "raining cats and dogs," one particular morning. My sister Simone and I gathered up some pots, pans, cups, bowls, and ran outside to collect as much rain water as our Heavenly Father would pour out to us. The reason we did this was because, well, the water was turned off again, and we saw an opportunity, to experiment in the midst of what looked like another jacked up situation. Fill by fill, we carried the loads of water into the kitchen and boiled the water, purifying it from any outside contaminations. You won't believe it but we were able to cook with the clean water, bathe, clean the house, though, not sure if we cleaned up, but still had more to use, if needed. Call us strange if you want, but that experience was a true eye opener as to how God already has the answers to the problems we are facing, if we just tune into His channel and not our own. To this day that situation still brings a smile to my face.

Back to being on trial for my straying away from God, and trying to lead my own life into my own desired destiny. I would've also been guilty of losing faith in God. Going to church with my family was always something we valued, whether it was with my mom and grandmother or learning how to praise God with staying with my dad and stepmom over the weekends. I mean, no offense to anyone who still does this today, but we would have to answer the phone by saying, "Praise the Lord, Aubrey's Residence." Sweet Jesus! I didn't want to be the one to answer the phone, because it felt uncomfortable at first, but then after the foolish butterflies flew away, I had fun saying it. My stepmom and dad went through this Pentecostal phase where we stayed underneath a tent church service, day and night, we kept the Sabbath Day holy, watched only Bible stories on TV and together, my five siblings and I had to learn the books of the Bible together. Talk about equipping us with the right tools to fight the warfare's we would soon have to face in our adult lives. To this day, my siblings and I still acknowledge how much we appreciate our parents for instilling such valuable character building skills within us.

Unfortunately, being raised between three different homes, my mom's, grandmother's and dad's, I had different parenting styles lingering all around me. What was a value and top priority for one household wasn't as important to the other, and vice versa. Conflicted, even as a young lady, I didn't like to talk much to people about what I felt internally, because well, I really never knew how that was to be done. I put on this shy persona, so that I wouldn't have to open up, even though I so desperately wanted and needed to. My mom and I had somehow had formed this mother-daughter relationship that looked more like buddies, minus the confiding in each other part. If I could go back to being that little girl or teenager, I would turn to my grandmother and ask her, "Why do I always feel like there is something different about me? Why do I feel like God has a calling on my life?"

I was a young Christian so I didn't even know what having a calling on your life even meant. I just thought that most people must've been plain right lucky in their lives, or skillfully talented, which provided a good living for them. I would lie on my grandmother's shoulder even more and ask, "Grandma, no matter how hard I try to disguise it, I don't seem to fit in with everyone else." If I had known what I know now, perhaps, I would have walked in my purpose much sooner.

Now that I am 29-years-old, journeying with God has been breathtaking, in the upmost exhilarating way. The maturity of my spirituality helps me to realize that God allowed me to go through my past experiences to draw me unto Him. See, it's one thing to rely on your parents' relationship with God, but it's another for you to form your own relationship with Him, willingly and on your own. God allows us to endure such hardships, not because He dislikes us, but because He loves us dearly. The trials and tribulations are meant to strengthen your faith, such as that of our beloved ancestors. And most importantly, Jesus endured much greater pain than all of us; *"For God so loved the world, that He gave His only begotten son, that whosoever believeth in Him should not perish but have ever lasting life."* (John 3:16 KJV)

Throughout this experience of spending time with me, my hope is that you find something you can relate to and rejoice over as we step into our greatness together. I encourage you not to look at the storms as discipline for your wrongdoings, but rather smile knowing that all trials have a lesson that's waiting to be discovered and revealed so that you can grow into the woman or man you were created to be. I started this journey with you by illustrating my courage to stand up against fear by stepping out of my own shackled comfort zone. Also, how fear has captivated our pure existence and crippled our ability to live the life that's called according to our purpose. Your setbacks are setups for a major comeback; I know you've heard this before right? Dispute knowing we all have pondered on the mind boggling question which never seems to go away, "Lord, how do I get to that place full of joy, happiness, peace, and contentment?"

Trust me, you're not alone, this was my cry out for a very long time. I'm cheerfully tickled because I'm super excited to share with you my journey and discoveries God revealed to me along the way. So! Are you ready? Go ahead and grab you a cup of coffee, or your cherry Kool-Aid pop, clear your mind from all distractions and let's set the atmosphere for a new perspective. We're going to journey together through the rough places, through the valleys, and through the dead zones. Not to fright along the way, but rather to stand firm because I will provide you with weapons to fight these battles with me. Trust me, we will need them. Don't take these weapons lightly for they will protect you. For the Bible says, *"The word is a lamp unto my feet and a light unto my path."* (Psalm 119:105 KJV).

Sharmetra Aubrey Lewis

Fighting Through Life's Lessons

When The Pressure Is On

"It is God who arms me with strength and makes my way perfect, He makes my feet like the feet of a deer; He enables me to stand on the heights."
- 2 Samuel 22:33-34 (NIV)

Lights, cameras, action! I remember back in high school, playing my favorite sport, basketball, it was the fourth quarter and the game was tied with one-minute to go. Hearts pounding, excessive sweat bursting from every pore of our tired bodies, because we ate too many hot chips from the day before, but the anxiety of winning and possibly losing the game gave us massive energy from within. The pressure was on to show what we were truly made of, especially since we had claimed to be strong and mighty, equipped for any battle. Comparing this frustrating experience to the challenges of life, I'm sure you can search your memory and find similar situations where you didn't see how in the world you were going to make it through life's obstacles. Life is all planned out, you got the man or wife, the kids, the house you wanted, and even looking good in the financial department. Yessssss! Brushing a chip off of your shoulder, you have no worries. You're not where you want to be, but thank God you're not where you used to be! Let's rejoice and give God the glory. Oh NO! Suddenly without warning, your world is shaken by a storm. Everything that comfortably seemed to be going well was snatched from you. Comfort zones, like a good paying job, lays you off; relationships turn sour; people who you once trusted, turn their backs on you; doors that were once opened have now been shut; the list goes on and on. You're left standing in this whirlpool of confusion and frustration, stress and agony, disappointment and shame, wondering, "Why God, is everything falling apart for me? What did I do to deserve this?"

This was my exact cry on February 15, 2008, when the pressure was on for me to woman up. Almost two years after graduating from high school I gave birth to a beautiful daughter Tori Lewis, on January 9, 2008, who happens to be a precious gem, wrapped in sparkling diamonds, and suited for her mission. The pressure wasn't from the birthing on my princess, but precisely hearing God's voice prior to the birth, telling me to give up trying to do things my way and move from Homer, LA to Dallas, TX with baby Tori. With my neck clenched tightly, teeth chattering, and a frightful but hopeful heart, I turned in my keys to my two-bedroom rent-free apartment. I moved in with my mom to prepare for Tori's arrival, so that afterwards baby Tori and I could relocate to Dallas, TX with my father. Eight months pregnant, I spent several nights sleeping on a solid concrete floor, on top of a five-inch mat, which protected baby Tori and I from the cold, solid foundation underneath us. I know you're probably wondering, why on earth would I do that? Well, still 19, young, dumb, and in love, I wanted to spend the last few nights I could with my then boyfriend, Tori's father, before we would have to leave him behind in Louisiana. See we had this whole thing planned out, so I thought. After I told him what God had spoken to me, his response was, "Gone and go to Texas, get established, and I will come too."

Five weeks after Baby Tori's arrival, my father was in town

to pick us up. As we loaded up the white Ford Expedition, I couldn't help but to wonder what was about to happen in our lives from that point forward. Final bags in the truck, car seat loaded and secured, kissing everyone goodbye, we began our journey to the unknown. Even though a part of me was excited for this new adventure, the other part was stuck from facing the distinct reality that I was going to be a single mom, when learning how to be a parent wasn't in the elementary through high school lesson plans.

My dad told me precisely, "Baby, it's you and Tori against the world."

Looking at him, I could see that he was speaking from a place of experience, but I wasn't ready to face that so-called reality for my life. As my fears unfolded, I was a single mom for five years, in a faraway land trying to figure out life as a young lady and how to be a mother. Now, if your face turned into a frown when you noticed that my child's father didn't honor his word, well keep journeying with you. Remember, I stated in the end God gets all the glory. As stubborn children, we oftentimes stand in our own way of His blessings. We like to stay resting in our comfort zones instead of rising into a higher dimension that aligns with our higher calling. So to make us move, God will start rocking and shaking things up in that comfort zone to awaken us and get our attention. He'll deter anything or anyone that nourishes us but does not completely satisfy us, causing us to seek His face because doing things without Him is not the way. So when the pressure is on, look at it as God's way of drawing the best out of you. The hell you go through is not meant to harm you, but instead it sets the stage for growth within you.

Molded For Perfection

When my daughter was as infant she was such a joy to look at, as she still is to this day. Despite the fact that everyone called her a gorgeous, juicy, cabbage patch, Gerber baby, because of her peach, juicy, soft cheeks, I admired her for other reasons. Reasons only a proud parent would noticeably consider positively unique and different, setting her apart from other babies. I tilt my hat to all babies, for they are so smart, learning very quickly how to adapt and grasp hold of survival mechanisms such as crawling, walking, talking, and Lord knows the countless others skills needed to adapt to a place outside of the mother's womb. These things a baby can learn very fast, but one in particular my baby girl found to not seem to have much importance to her. Instead of crawling, using both hands and knees, like an average baby, my daughter acted as if her two knees were allergic to touching the floor after a few months. You should've seen her! I say this jokingly, but she moved around like she was part of the ape family, with her posture tilted forward but using feet to walk instead of knees. This was her crawling/walking stance. She decided very quickly that crawling on her knees was not what she wanted to do very long. To all other infants 6-7 months of age, this type of crawling screamed CONFUSING, but to my baby girl, this was her comfortable norm. And don't get it twisted, she was rolling with speed as she set out on her path towards destruction and curiosity throughout the house.

I bet you're probably wondering what am I getting at by sharing with you this weird story? Or if you're like me, you're trying to figure out things ahead of time. You may have thought, maybe she's getting at how you can operate in dysfunction for so long, that doing things dysfunctional can become the only way you know how to function. Not bad, if you concluded that, but what I am showing you is how God instills in us gifts, talents, and certainly passions, even before we can begin to recognize it. We couldn't quite figure out how walking forward like an ape was understandably appropriate, but maybe my daughter knew even as a child that she had the gift of being strong, flexible, and courageous. Courageous enough to try the unknown despite what everyone said and what the other babies did around her. The way she decided to walk was not tied to the way others viewed how walking should be illustrated. She was led by her own internal spiritual guidance. Needless to say, my baby was walking like you and I before she was nine months old. It was the cutest visual to look at, seeing a 9-month-old baby, with short juicy but strong legs, tiptoeing around everywhere. No longer was she stretched forward like an ape, but instead walking upright with stronger limbs than a 2-year-old. She's an incredible gymnast, with outstanding flexibility, tumbling skills, and coordination. Now 10 years old, she still loves to position her body in awkward positions and never seems to get enough of flipping.

Recognizing that God has gifted her with such skills forced

me to look back and examine my own life. As I reflect, I meditated deeply over the things that may have seemed to slip through the cracks and maybe went unnoticed or brushed off as not being that big of a deal. They suddenly became my **AH HA MOMENTS**!

AH HA! That's why I was so chatty and friendly, because God knew that my bubbly personality would someday align with my soul's purpose in order to fulfill my destiny. AH HA! That's why I loved to play school when I was a kid, because God knew that being a teacher was what I would someday become. Even the painful experiences of life carried AH HA moments, because through the pain, God developed a character in me that could not have been established if I had not gone through what I went through. Through the pain I gained patience, courage, resilience, wisdom, humility, character, and so much more. Look back over your life. What are some events or moments in your life that always seem to resurface, but in a way that benefits you? If you're uncertain, then ask someone very close to you, maybe a family member, your best friend, or a spouse, what they see in you. Nine times out of ten, someone else will see the things that you seem to overlook or write off as not being anything spectacular. That very skill, characteristic, gift or passion, could be where your treasure lies. God knew who we were and who you are to become, even in your mother's womb. So, slow down and pay attention to all of life's experiences, because in them hold the truth to who you really are.

REFLECTION

1.) What are some things about you that seem uniquely different and everyone seems to notice it?

_____
_____
_____
_____

2). What are some characteristics about yourself that seems to annoy others and yourself?

_____
_____
_____
_____

3). What are some characteristics about yourself that seems to make people appreciate you?

_____
_____
_____
_____

4). Try doing new things and keep a record of what interests you. God will use new experiences to reveal to you more of who you are and who you are not. What have you learned about yourself?

_____
_____
_____
_____
_____

Smile In The Midst of

"Though the mountains be shaken and the hills be removed, yet my unfailing love for you will not be shaken nor my covenant of people be removed," says the Lord, who has compassion on you.
- Isaiah 54:10 (NIV)

How often do you see yourself smiling or feeling your soul overflowing with joy? Ask yourself if you only smile to the people that you like, love and trust, or when something extraordinary happens to you? If you answered yes to these questions, then it's okay. My goal is to get you to see that it's acceptable to rejoice in the midst of rainy days, because even in the rain God is still with you. My soul began to rejoice at the countdown of a New Year. To make one full year as a single mom, I was delighted to see what the next year would bring. I couldn't wait to explore the horizons, to set New Year resolutions, as if I ever kept any, but at least the anticipations was exciting! My heart was boldly convinced that 2009 would be better than 2008. What I didn't know was that a devastating storm was right around the corner, ready to strike like a lightening volt turned up to the max. Still secretly depressed from my plans of having my family together not evolving, my body began to reveal to me that something was deeply troubling it early in 2009. Like many people, I ignored the signals and kept on focusing on being a good mother and trying to figure out this thing called parenting. Playing house and with Barbie's as a kid did not do a good job of preparing me for this unpredictable lifestyle. My parents need to get a refund. Demanding my attention, the signals and symptoms that something was not right in my body screamed louder and louder. Still stubborn, as the most stubborn animal on earth, I treated the symptoms by feeding it what it demanded. For instance, when I was extremely thirsty, I would drink everything under the sun to try and quench my unquenchable thirst. When my bladder filled excessively, I would release it providing room for more to be stored. When I felt fatigue, I would find myself tucked inside of a blanket, laying around, lacking energy to move about. I just thought I had grown lazy, since I didn't have friends or anything to do in Texas; I was a long way from home. I realized this wasn't right when I unwillingly lost 10-15 pounds in a week, and my tongue was as white as snowflakes and as sticky as an angry teacher's chalkboard.

At last! I had made up in my mind that I was going to see a doctor, well, after I had gotten my braces installed on my teeth. Girl! Are you insane?! Yes, I was the insane chick, who after all of what was going on I still wanted to go correct my two front teeth because I hated it all of my life and now could finally afford to pay for it. Sitting in the dentist chair, I could tell this experience was not about to go as I anticipated. I could feel the fatigue sensation smothering my soul while dark black circles covered both my eyes. "Are you ok?" the dentist asked as the assistant hurried off to get me a small cup of water. I must've had dehydration written all over me or perhaps my mouth was dryer than a Sahara Desert. For crying out loud, gulping down the water was a mistake. My body hit the reversal button and all but the stomach itself came gushing out. My body had had enough and was no longer playing by my rules; it was time to go seek help. The completion of the braces install was postponed; I decided it was time to go the ER, no more delaying, and no more denying that I had a serious issue. Now, a wise person would've asked for an ambulance to transport them, but being a single mom created in me this 'do it myself don't ask for any help' insane mentality, that could have cost me my life, literally. Luckily, the hospital was a few blocks from the dental office, but the condition I gradually fell in was frightening. Driving towards the hospital, my vision began to blur, everything seemed to collide together. I couldn't tell if the traffic light was red, yellow, green, or purple, I was just driving recklessly, so I thought. My strength began to fade so drastically, that I had to lean on the driver's window for support. Struggling to take a deep breath, I whispered, "Lord, I need you!" I knew I was in big trouble and I couldn't do this on my own strength. The Lord must really love me because my prayer was answered, and I safely arrived to the ER without killing myself, any other drivers, or pedestrians along the way. Now, the next challenge was getting in there. I stumbled to the check-in and was immediately seen by a nurse, who could tell I severely needed help. As part of my vital signs, my blood glucose level was tested, which changed my life forever.

The nurse brought the doctor back into the room where the two looked at me and asked, "Who drove you here?"

Confused, but knowing why they may have asked, I whispered between the shortness of breath, "I did."

Quietness filled the atmosphere for a moment, until the nurse questioned, "Sweetie, how old are you?"

Fearing what the results revealed, I softly spoke, "I'm 21, why do you ask?"

With compassion in her heart she let the doctor speak, "You're a Type 1 Diabetic and your blood glucose level has reached a level that can be deadly if we don't get you treated right away."

"I'm, I'mmmm a what?" I frighteningly asked, thinking back to the severity of my great-grandmother's diabetes and how it along with reoccurring strokes claimed her life. "How much sugar did I have?" immaturely asking as if they had it poured up in a measuring cup.

Baffled as to how I was still walking around and not somewhere laid over dead, the doctor said, "Your blood sugar is far beyond the normal highs. It's more around the 1,000 range, which means that your bloodstream is like maple syrup."

The nurse shook her head in agreement adding, "Some diabetics fall into a diabetic coma with highs much less than yours."

I didn't care to hear that I was close to facing a diabetic coma, but I was grateful for God sparing my life. I immediately felt like Shadrach, Meshach, and Abednego, the three Jews who refused to worship the image of gold that King Nebuchadnezzar had set up. Furiously heating the furnace seven times hotter than usual, he tied them up and had them thrown in. But after rejoicing for a little while, the King noticed there were not three, but four men walking around in the furnace, unbound and unharmed. The fourth man happened to look like the son of God. You can read this for yourself in the Book of Daniel Chapter 3. I'm a believer that God will shield you in the midst of any storm. A tragedy that may take out someone else, may be the very one that God covers you in. And in the midst of protecting you, He'll reveal Himself to you and to everyone else around you. Smile in the midst of your storm, for out of your storm He gets the glory.

Rock Bottom

If the lord delights in a man's way, he makes
his steps firm; though he stumble, he will not fall,
for the lord upholds him with his hand.
- Psalm 37:23-24 (NIV)

As I reflect back over my life, I realize that I have been knocked down a thousand times, multiplied by a thousand more times, so it seems. It's funny how when you're in high school, your plans for the future seem perfect and ideal, suitable for who you are and what you feel you're worth. Never do you think that struggling, being broke, or failing will be tagging along with you throughout your life's journey. Not for the long haul at least. I remember standing in Biology class, my senior year in high school, with a few classmates, who were all discussing what their plans were after graduation. One friend said she was going to be a neurologist, because she loved how dynamic the brain was so she wanted to explore it too. Another said with the biggest smile spreading across her pretty, yellow face, "I'm going to be a physical therapist, so that I can help rehabilitate people!" As I looked down from the second floor of our dirty classroom window, I couldn't help but to swallow the agony of future fears that haunted me. That fear that sat dormant inside of me, waiting to resurrect was that I would struggle, not finish college, and be poor for the rest of my life. Seeing the university everyone else was choosing to attend, I made the mental commitment that I was going to follow my friends to the same university so that we could stick together while pursuing our dreams. At least I felt this would buy me some time until I figured out what I wanted to do with my life. I honestly didn't know what I was going to go to college for, or what type of preparation I needed beforehand. The furthest my eyes could see was getting my high school diploma and making my grandmother proud of me. Knowing that grandma struggled to finish high school, because she had to take care of her elderly sick parents, motivated me to achieve it successfully for the both of us. After graduating from high school and stepping out into the real world, I fell flat on my face. It was like walking confidently down a flight of stairs then immediately missing a step. Boom! Nothing seemed to work out for me, I moved from city to city, state to state, searching for peace, peace I could not find. Schools I attended, I either quit or flunked course after course. I searched for answers in all the wrong people and made excuses to justify my mistakes. Can you imagine the scars from all of those nasty falls? After realizing that I had no clue how to get myself out of the mess, I finally let go and let God take the wheel. Comforting my lost soul, He reminded me to depend on Him and not myself. See God gives us choices and free will, but those choices doesn't exempt us from the consequences of our actions. Many will travel in the opposite direction of God's will and wind up doing things that are so far from who God calls them to be. Another important key factor is to realize that not all falls are because you are going against God's will, but they're obstacles He uses to mold and sculpt you into His beautiful preplanned masterpiece.

The good thing about our Father is that He is the master in control of your destiny. No matter how you begin your journey, God controls the beginning and the ending, if only you follow His lead. See I know for a fact that God has purposely allowed me to fall time and time again so that I could humbly see that He is the head over my life and that I cannot fulfill my divine purpose without Him.

Tears
    Are
        Water
           For
              The
                  Garden
                  Of
                      Victory!!

Lessons Learned

Perseverance must finish its work so that you may be mature and complete, not lacking anything.
- James 1:4 (NIV)

Have you ever wondered why you go through what you go through? No matter what your parents or loved ones, with some sense, tell you you still don't take it into consideration. You figure that you have it all worked out. "Thanks for the advice or concern but I got this," you say with your head held high and your chest stuck out like Superman because, well, you got this right? Then, what do you know, suddenly without warning, invitation, or preparation, disaster strikes. You now have to look the people you rejected counsel from in the eyes, only to hear, "I told you so!" Sweet mother of God, those four words aligned together only aggravate you so much, because you know if only you had listened life would've been much easier. I used to question God for allowing me to experience such pains and upset in my life. Heck, I even had enough anger to punch a hole in the wall when I failed the same tests over and over again. Test me again, I'm ready now! It's like taking an open book test, with provided answers, but scoring a zero numerous of times.

Now that my walk with Christ is strengthened by His word, I'm able to see more clearly with my spiritual eyes, which were once blurred. See what I didn't understand was how the flesh and the spirit were so opposite of each other. I didn't realize that if I fully allowed the Holy Spirit to guide me, then I wouldn't be quickly lead by my own sinful cravings and desires. For the Word says, "So I say, walk by the Spirit, and you will not gratify the desires of the flesh. For the flesh desires what is contrary to the Spirit, and the Spirit what is contrary to the flesh. They are in conflict with each other, so that you are not to do whatever[a] you want (Galatians 5:16-17 NIV).

Many of us have to experience things on our own in order to understand what someone else was trying to tell us all along. Even though God uses other people to cover and protect us, He sits back and allows us to experience hell on our own, in hopes that we learn a valuable lesson. If that lesson isn't learned, you will find yourself experiencing the same thing all over again, while wondering to yourself, "What's really going on?" "Or am I really this stupid to keep doing this over and over?" Please don't get discouraged and ready to throw in the towel when you go through such traumatic storms, instead chose to see it as God's way of training His warrior for the battles to come. Life's lessons are the best teacher of life. There's a purpose in every pain, every tear cried, and every heart broken that you experience. Out of life's experiences comes wisdom and growth because it brings about the knowledge of God, understanding of truth, and the ability to share your blessing with someone else.

On the next page I ask that you think deeply about a lesson you had to repeat but has made you become a better person once the lesson was learned.

REFLECTION

1). What lessons have you found yourself repeating time and time again?

_____
_____
_____
_____

2). What did you learn from that mistake that has made you a better person?

_____
_____
_____
_____

3). How did you handle those situations differently?

_____
_____
_____
_____

4). What will be your advice to someone else who may be experiencing similar troubles?

_____
_____
_____
_____

Seek Wisdom

> Wisdom makes one wise man more powerful than ten
> rulers in a city.
> - Ecclesiastes 7:19 (NIV)

It really amazes me how we were taught that wisdom comes with age, but the longer I exist the more I realize how untrue that statement is. The dictionary defines wisdom as the ability to discern or judge what is true, right or lasting. I've heard wisdom and knowledge get tossed around interchangeably as if they are the same, but even I know they are not. Knowledge is defined as the information gained from experiences and reasoning. However, the great thing about wisdom and knowledge is that they can work hand in hand with one another. I read one example that said knowledge is like knowing how to use a gun, but wisdom is knowing when to use it and when to put it away. To distinguish the differences try studying the Book of Proverbs, for I found this to be the best place in the Bible to gain a better understanding of wisdom. (Proverbs 1: 7 NIV) says, "The fear of the LORD is the beginning of knowledge, but fools despise wisdom and instructions."

My beautiful grandmother is a phenomenal example of a woman of wisdom. Grandma Eliza, named after her grandmother Elizabeth, shows both knowledge and wisdom. Being a single mother of four, with an inactive father who abandoned her, she never showed signs of turning away from God. My grandmother was and still is the hardest working woman known by man, to ever step foot on this majestic green earth. She faithfully dedicated 20 plus years to job that didn't pay much nor did the employer have any consideration to life's inflation rates. Talk about an eagle mounting others up on her wings, my grandmother played a big role in raising me and all of my siblings, clothing us, feeding us, putting money in our pockets, and getting us all through high school. I remember hopping in the car when she went to Piggly Wiggly, the local grocery store or to Pack A Bag, one of the town's corner store because I knew whatever I asked for grandma would buy for me. "Grandma, can I have these chips," I would ask, knowing the answer would be yes.

She always smiled, lifting her high round cheekbones, the ones like I have, answering, "Put what you want in the buggy." You may call buggies shopping carts in the city, but in the country they're just buggies. It always puzzled me how a woman so alone, with limited income, and no child support from a man, could take care of so many people, pay her bills on time, tithe faithfully, and yet still have more stored up for the rainy days. When I finally built up the courage to ask grandma how she was able to do so much, I expected her to spill the beans and admit that she has some sort of secretive boyfriend, who was her outside provider. Needless to say, her response certainly acknowledged the providing lover in her life. Grandma smiled at me with twinkling eyes and proclaimed, "God is my provider." She then went on to say, "I haven't' always been this relaxed, certain, and fearless in the midst of my circumstances. In fact, I used to worry and stress about how I was going to make ends meet, I thought I couldn't handle it."

Nodding my head, I could definitely relate to that.

She went on to say, "But the longer I went through the storm, the better my understanding was of God and my understanding of Him fully developed."

Grandma had the wisdom to understand that no matter the challenges of life, as long as she stayed trusting in the Word, truth, life, and abundance would be made available to all.

You may not have a grandparent in your life who can guide you with both knowledge and wisdom, but open your heart to receive wisdom. The scripture says, "If any of you lack wisdom, you should ask God, who gives generously to all without finding fault and it will be given to you. (James 1:5 NIV). Wisdom will protect you in the midst of adversities. It's a light that never fades, but continues to grow brighter, stronger and stronger. I encourage you today to pray and seek God's wisdom and you will live a life full of joy and happiness too.

"WISDOM SEPARATES A WISE MAN FROM A FOOL"

Rejoice Anyhow

Let us not be weary in doing good, for at the proper
time will reap a harvest if we do not give up.
- Galatians 6:9 (NIV)

Rejoice in your present situation for out of the storm comes nourishment to grow. Shall we look at how nature's thin, translucent, green grass glow in the sunlight or how colorful, diligent, and light-hearted flowers are able to become the beautiful background for our earthy foundation. How do you think these abundant present creations are able to blossom and sprout such structured characteristics? Perhaps it's the fertilizer casted upon their amazing roots or its God's showers that reach beneath their roots and pulls greatness up and through them. They do not complain at the thought of being washed away or drenched during the storm, instead they rejoice knowing that the storm is only God's way of providing them with the strength they need to carry on with life. Isn't that exactly like our precious lives today?

God allows us to go through such terrifying storms in order to bless us and to push forth a blessing through us. Adversities are not meant to harm us, but to build character within us. May 2013, I didn't know how on earth I would be able to rejoice again. With diabetes severely causing infectious vulnerability to my body, I somehow attracted an infection that almost killed me. I found myself faced with the

45

decision to either surgically remove my fallopian tubes and right ovaries, or try to remove the gigantic cysts that held my body hostage and pray they never returned. The choice to do what was right, came with an enormous price, one I was not ready to pay, not in this lifetime nor another.

Tears flooding my soul and sorrow internally smothering me minute by minute when I decided to have the surgery, which as a result left me internally scarred for life. I went years silently crying as I thought of not being able to conceive a child ever again. I felt washed out, as if my parade had been rained on permanently and that I wasn't good enough for my husband anymore. Negative self-chatter was talking me out of being who I was in the sight of God and it was trying to destroy me. Standing in faith, I began trusting in His word.

Not only was I able to overcome that burdened pain, but giving it to Jesus, I was able to regain my strength and sanity once more. I may not be able to bear children again, but the physical limitation does not limit my heartfelt ability to love and care for other children. As a matter of fact, thanks to my inability to conceive, I've discovered my passionate purpose when it comes to emerging myself into instilling valuable skills into every child around me. Intertwining both my pain and love for children has pushed and pulled me closer towards my destiny. Having such a heartfelt connection to children, I believe is what helps make me to be the great schoolteacher that I am today. See the fire that burns us, not only hurts temporarily, but strengthens us all at once. It springs forth the hidden jewels within us that would not have been discovered had we not gone through what we went through. Job 13:15 (NIV) says, *"Though he slay me, yet will I hope in him; I will surely defend my ways to his face."*

46

I smile at the empathy I'm able to sincerely give to young women who are going or have gone through similar difficulties. I'm also reminded that He blessed me with a beautiful daughter and a stepson, who were sent to me for me to love as my own. Psalm 119:71 I love for it says, *"It was good for me to be afflicted so that I may learn your decrees."*

Whatever your situation is today, smile and rejoice knowing that out of your adversities come opportunities; opportunities to be blessed and opportunities to be a blessing to someone else. Share the good news, enjoy the current circumstance, and appreciate all that God is doing for you and through you. Don't hide your joy beneath your sadness but instead frighten the devil by letting your light shine in midst of the storm. Think of happiness as a contagious sickness. The more you rejoice, the more others catch hold of your airborne virus. The infectious praise of the righteous will drown out any evil.

The Oppression Of Fear

> "Be strong and courageous. Do not be afraid or terrified because of them, for the lord your God goes with you; He will never leave you nor forsake you."
> - Deuteronomy 31:6 (NIV)

Why is it that we are so powerful in our minds, but weak when it comes to our actions? We're really good at speaking great plans but hide beneath a rock when it's time to actually apply them to our lives. It seriously makes you question, who is this selfish person that is stopping me from reaching higher altitudes? What ungrateful person is blocking the entry way to my success? If you're decidedly trying to figure out who would do such a selfish thing, let me just go ahead and tell you to stop wasting your time on trying to blame other people. You no longer have to be in denial of the fact that you are the reason you cannot move forward in your life. See, fear dwells within us like a fetus in a mother's womb. It attaches itself to anyone that feeds into its growth. Fear tells you that you're not good enough or that the things desired most are not for you. I encourage you to find that leader within yourself. Search for that roaring lion within YOU. It's in there, it's just waiting on you to uncage it. Finding it will require that you do some self-reflecting though, and it requires that you trust your struggle, knowing that it will be for your greater good. What sucks is how in this information age that we live in is so detrimental to our authenticity. Social media platforms like; Facebook, Instagram, Snapchat, Twitter, and Lord knows what else now, controls the imagery of our perception of life. Feeling like we have to compare ourselves to others feeds our inner deepest fears and insecurities that it creates social anxiety and dysfunction. Abraham says the best way to predict the future is to create it. Instead of living life according to God's calling, we imprison ourselves with fear, competition, jealously, or comfort. I thought getting a good paying corporate job was succeeding, but really it was my comforting prison.

Yep, I said it! See my prison was sitting silently inside my tiny, four foot tall box called a cubicle, wondering what was my reason for going to college, getting a Dental Assistant Certification, Life Insurance License, Associate of Science and a Bachelor of Psychology Degree, to only sit for nine hours a day, staring at a computer screen, pushing numbers all day. I knew I was a social butterfly, who enjoyed helping people, but working in the mortgage industry was one of my comfort zones that paid the bills and kept the lights on. I was always excited to flee the building at 4:27 p.m. on the dot, only to be stuck sitting in rush hour traffic for an additional hour. That comfort zone gave me enough time to run pick my baby up from school, prepare dinner for the family, assist with homework, do laundry, shut my eyes to wind down, only to be wakened by the ruthless annoying alarm clock at 5:15 a.m. to do it all over again. Ugh, make it stop!

It amazes me at how this daily routine has become the norm for so many people. Those who are not stuck in a trance, but living their lives doing what they are passionate about, are looked at as if they have some sort of super power that makes them extraordinary. I learned from my favorite author and transformational speaker, Lisa Nichols, that calling someone else extraordinary is an excuse to let yourself off the hook. Instead of accepting extraordinary, she explains that she is not extraordinary, but instead chooses to make extraordinary decisions. Talk about golden nuggets! Those are some powerful words right there. I want to also choose to make extraordinary decisions. We don't have to sacrifice our freedom, paid by the blood of the lamb, only to lay aside our dreams in order to live a life full of abundance.

It would be selfish of me to say that those who are living the American dream deserves it, but the truth of the matter is, they earned it. As I self-reflect over my life, I realize that being paralyzed to a life beneath God's calling was my own choice. Whether consciously or unconsciously, we are sculpting our own realities, no one else is to blame. No one is forcing us to do what the masses are doing or hide behind what seems to be job security, in hopes that God comes where we are. Instead, we have to trust in His word wholeheartedly, for the word says in Roman 8:28, "And we know that in all things God works for the good of those who love him, who have been called according to his purpose."

My challenge for you today, is that you really put into perspective what God is calling you to do, right where you are. If what you are doing does not line up with your gifts, passion or calling, ask yourself these three questions:

- What can I do to use my gifts right where I am?
- What lessons are for me to learn during this season?
- How can I align my purpose and passion with your calling to create a better opportunity for myself and others?

Instead of becoming depressed over where you are right now, these questions will interrupt your habitual thought patterns, and force you to focus on different questions. After all, different questions, yield different answers, which will bring forth different results in your life.

"NEVER LET THE FEAR OF STRIKING OUT KEEP YOU FROM PLAYING THE GAME."

REFLECTION

1). What are my biggest fears that are keeping me from living my dream life?

_____
_____
_____
_____

2). What qualities do I need to obtain in order to be the person God has called me to be?

_____
_____
_____
_____

3). If I was not afraid to live full out, who and what would I be doing with my life right now?

_____
_____
_____
_____

4). When do I want to make the change and break free?

_____
_____
_____
_____

Don't Settle For Less

My spirit became terribly disturbed as I reflected over the moments where I intentionally allowed doors that were opened to shut in my face because I was afraid to walk through to the other side. Although I strayed from God's calling numerous of times, I chuckle because the run-away caused me to settle for less. What a douche bag right! Instead of believing that I am a true heir to the inheritance of the king, I allowed other people's opinion to persuade me into believing what God had promised for me. I remember skimming through job postings searching only for careers that I knew would be easy for me, while avoiding those that challenged every part of me. I would read the job descriptions of what of it took to be a qualified candidate and say to myself, "Nope, I can't do that," or "Whelps, I'm not ready for that at this stage of my life." I would use some well-rehearsed outdated excuse to back me up like, "When I get my college degree, then I'll be ready."

One of my dear friends I met years ago reminded me why it is important to live life to the fullest. See, before her dad passed, his final words to his loving daughter were, "Live your to the fullest." Her dad lost himself in worrying about pleasing everyone else, that he never took the time to sit and ask himself, "What is my life all about?"

I know I am not the only one who has talked themselves out of a wonderful opportunity because of that little voice in the back of our mind causing us to doubt ourselves. So instead of reaching for the crown, you reached for a headband and watched everyone else around you go after their dreams and ambition. That's why I am here to remind you that as God's children, we all inherit His wealth. Being heirs to the kingdom means that there's nothing that we cannot have or ask for that will not be granted to us on earth. There is no request too large or too small for you if you decree it. Job 22:28 says, "What you decide on will be done, and light will shine on your ways."

Dream big and dare to have more for it already has your name on it.

FIGHTING FOR RELATIONSHIPS

That's My Best Friend

"Oooo, girl, I have thousands of friends on Facebook and Instagram!"

"Look, such and such are following me and XYZ liked my picture I posted this morning!"

Does that sound familiar? How many of you have people in your life, better yet strangers, you call friends? I have a boatload of so-called friends, I couldn't count on to rub two pennies together to save my life, so I'm guilty too. If I was a Merriam-Webster dictionary, I would be crying and stomping all over this new day and age definition of the word friend. How about? Let's pretend for a second, I'm a Webster dictionary. I would present to you the word friend, defined as, 'a person who has strong liking for and trust in another.' Or better yet, I'll show you who you really are. I'll tell you a friend is someone who is not your enemy, but instead someone that's a favored companion. Whelp that eliminates two-thirds of my so-called friends in a matter of 1.23 seconds.

When I think of a true friend, I look at the relationship Mary and Elizabeth had together. You can follow their Twitter relationship more in Luke Chapter 1 versus 39-45. Yes, they were relatives but that's beside the point. When Mary needed someone to confide in, whom she could trust, she turned to Elizabeth. Now, I'm sure after the angel Gabriel had shared that she would be conceiving a child in her old age she could've discussed this with someone else living in her own village. Instead, she must've realized that just because people claim to love you don't mean they have your best interest at heart. Even on my own journey, I've learned, through mishaps, to be careful who I share my visions with. Another thing I took from Mary's and Elizabeth's friendship, was unconditional love for each other's blessings. Elizabeth could've easily been jealous of Mary; for conceiving the Son of God. After all, the angel did appear to Zechariah, Elizabeth's husband, first. I can see the bitterness now, if I told my friend/cousin that I am going to be pregnant with the Son of God and that her baby is going to serve mines. Even if Elizabeth liked my baby bump photos on Facebook, Instagram, and Snapchat, deep down, I knew she would've been hating on me. But their relationship was genuine.

A real friendship should feel like a brother or sister, which you longed to have. Real friends will never abuse or misuse you, but delight themselves in lifting you up. A real friend tells you the truth. They may not always agree with every decision you make, but they support you anyways. Unlike societies meaning of "friends with benefits", a true friend with benefits comes with the perks of loyalty, support, trustworthiness, respect, and a lasting shoulder to cry on. If you have someone who's quick to gossip about your failures, instead of lending a helping hand, he or she is not your true friend. Choose wisely who you run with, for they can take you down faster than the Titanic or elevate you to higher heights. I've learned that when choosing my social circle, to choose people who stirred in the direction of my future and not my past. Place yourself around people who want as much out of life as you do. If you don't, you'll find yourself talking with so-called friends, only to realize that you're having a conversation with yourself.

Have this ever happened to you? You were trying so hard to fit into a certain group, only to notice y'all have absolutely nothing in common anymore? Your views on life were on a whole new level, but theirs were still stuck where you used to be? Awkward huh? It's not the end of the world though. As you look to reevaluate your circle, keep in mind your future and not your past. Who you were is not who you are or who you will become, so like O.T. Genesis says, "You need to cut it!" Remember, friendship is something that should be earned. Everyone won't be privileged to receive it. Guard your benefits.

FRIENDSHIP IS AN INVESTMENT.

Top 5 Traits of Friendship

- Trustworthiness
- Honesty
- Dependability
- Loyalty
- The Ability to Trust Others

REFLECTION

1). How many personal friends do you have in your life?

_____

_____

_____

_____

2). Do you see everyone on your social media accounts as true friends? Why or why not?

_____

_____

_____

_____

3). What does it take for you to make and keep a real friend?

_____

_____

_____

_____

4). In what ways have you shown you were a good friend?

_____

_____

_____

_____

5). What are some additional qualities needed to be a friend of yours?

_____

_____

_____

_____

Honor God Not Man

Jesus said, "Seek first his kingdom and his righteousness and all these things will be given unto you as well."
- Matthew 6:33 (NIV)

We have tried so hard to please the men and women in our world by doing any and everything for them. We have spent a lifetime trying to convince them that we are what they need and desire, even if it includes giving up our own identity and creating a falsified replica of what we are not. There's no other way to say it other than "Being Fake", not being true to who we really are. Trying to keep up with the Jones, we'll go broke buying fake hair that cost enough to pay two months mortgage. From eyelashes, fake nails, bleached skin color, liposuction, fake luxurious lifestyles that's all established off of credit just to impress other people. Don't get me wrong, I love my hair weaves and sew-ins, but we begin settling for what man thinks is acceptable and forget that we once had our own morals and standards. We can stop with the fakeness, manipulations, and dishonor because there's only one man who matters in our life. The one who sees perfection in our imperfection. The Bible says in Genesis 1:31, "God saw all that He had made, and behold, it was very good." We should not meet standards for other people because in God's eyes we are the perfect candidates.

I encourage you to stop stepping out of character, surrendering yourself with people who don't know who you are, and living your life according to the ways of the world. Honor God because He is the only significant other that can give you the love and respect you deserve. Make a commitment with me today that you will live to love and honor God first, because He is longing to build a loving relationship with you,

LORD
I
LOVE
YOU!

The Result Of Being Positive

To those who by persistence in doing good seek glory, honor and immortality, he will give eternal life.
- Romans2:7 (NIV)

Positive thinking is beginning to gain more attention than it has, particularly when it comes to creating the life you desire. Now, we can admit that positive thinking alone does not magically give you the results of success, as much as taking massive actions does. But, what positive thinking does is it raises your vibrations, allowing you to attract the things that you desire most. Having positive thoughts and beliefs are the most powerful keys to the law of attraction. What is this thing called the law of attraction? Well, I'm glad you asked! The law of attraction simply states that we don't attract what we want, but who we are. Have you ever noticed that whenever you carry around this nasty attitude, negative energy follows you, causing negative experiences to occur? Funny thing, while writing about this topic I was being tested. Going about my day as a dental assistant, everything was fine, I couldn't ask for a more peaceful experience. All of sudden, out of nowhere, I was knocked off my high horse, with a sprinkle of bitterness somehow lurking the atmosphere. I had to deal with bashful attitudes, people angry for no reason, dental exams driving me up the wall, with a chainsaw chasing after my innocent but annoyed soul.

It was over, like an evil witch's spell, I began consuming the energy from everyone else around me. Everything I tried to do from that point had the poorest results. My body's posture was so slouched, I came off as the unwelcoming dental assistant who didn't want to be bothered. Instead of leaving my awful experience at work, I took it all home with me and apparently unleashed its negative presence in the house. My husband seemed angry, we couldn't seem to agree on anything, dinner didn't come out right, and ugh I just wanted this awful day to end. What started out as a smile turned into an ugly frown. I tried to analyze how a day full of such joy turned into a living nightmare. Trying to get back to that positive state of mind, I silently repeated these comforting words, "No weapon formed against me shall prosper." As those words began to resonate in my heart, I immediately began to feel lifted by a more positive frequency that began attracting more positive experiences for me. See I learned through practicing positive thinking that it can help you manifest more love, joy, more money, abundance, better health, freedom, and so much more.

Although there's darkness around you, it doesn't have the power over you...

STAY POSITIVE

Mistreating Others

"Do unto others as you will have them to do unto you."
- Matthew 7:12 (NIV)

God, you are so gracious enough to look beyond our faults and see all of our needs, I love how He saw that the world He created needed to redeem from sin. Showing mercy on us He selected our dear Mary to give birth to Jesus, our savior, who came and sacrificed His life for us. Jesus, who knew no sin, took on sin so that He may blend in with all others around Him. From the outside looking in, one would have thought Jesus was a broke, homeless man, like the ones we see on the streets daily. Although He appeared to not be wealthy, He was the king of kings, lord of lords, and the son of the most high. He may not even have been very appealing in His fashioned attire, or material possessions, but the calling over His life radiated the earth, capturing the hearts of many. He was the perfect gentleman to those who didn't believe in Him, who mocked, and abused Him. People were jealous of Him because they didn't understand Him or because they found no way of relating to Him. They did whatever they could think of to get rid of Him, removing Him from their selfish presence.

Oh but thank God, this was all in the master's plan! Are you guilty of looking over or despising people because they do not fit your description of what looks good? I mean seriously think about it. Can you recall a time when you turned your nose up at someone who had a horrendous odor, wore dirty clothes, or wasn't very attractive to you? Or perhaps, they made less money than you and drove an outdated car that didn't sit well next to the one you park in your fabulous two-car garage nightly? Be careful who you mistreat for karma has a funny way of circling back around to you. You just never know who you are mistreating because remember God sits high and looks low and He sees our every move and know the desires of our hearts. As a matter of fact, I'm almost certain that the least among us could be an angel in disguise, testing your spiritual growth. Matthew 25:40 says, "The King will reply, 'Truly I tell you, whatever you did for one of the least of these brothers and sisters of mine, you did for me." Be careful my loved ones not to miss out on your blessings.

Detach 2 Reattach

Create in me a pure heart, O God and renew a steadfast
spirit within me.
- Psalm 51:10 (NIV)

Isn't it obvious that when we hook up with something
or someone that is not of God, life dwindles on a downward
path? We become worshipers to our own fleshly distractions,
submitting ourselves to unacceptable lifestyles. The scripture
reminds us that, "When tempted, no one should say, "God
is tempting me." For God cannot be tempted by evil, nor
does He tempt anyone; but each person is tempted when
they are dragged away by their own evil desire and enticed.
(James 1:13-14 NIV) It brought sadness to my soul, as I
listened to my friends' season of pain she had to endure,
due to being connectedly drawn to the wrong person. See
my friend committed her love and affection to a beautiful,
well-kept book, before carefully examining its inner deepest
context. She fell in love with a man, whose love that she
felt was as equal to that of Romeo and Juliet. Blinded by
love, what she couldn't see was Satan trying to destroy her
through the man she so desired. His relationship with God
was more than verbal that it was visible, he used God's
word to enslave her, making her captive by his unholy mind
games.

She began to lose sight of everything that was important
in her life and the lives of her children. Addicting her to

crack cocaine, she began submitting her body to explicit sexual behaviors, conning people for money, stealing and deceiving others to gain more and more. Out of love she endured painful beatings, as an expression of her love and weakness to desire more. Everything she worked hard for, was snatched away right before her eyes, leaving her broken and empty. Her honorable reputation, of being the sweetest, caring, warm-hearted woman was fractured, replaced by a negative visual and dispersal of unpleasant, unladylike information. She became a drug addict, feeding into its temporary fulfillment, with hopes that all her problems would somehow fade away.

Trying to get it together was a battle that she could not seem to get a grip on. As a result, her children were removed from her care and everything was lost. There seemed to be nothing worth fighting for, but oh how God has a way of turning things around. Reaching out and embracing her with His comforting arms, He fed her soul with his complete love and affection. She reclaimed back her life by choosing life and not death. She detached from what was dragging her away from God and instead took off running towards Him. Her joy and happiness was once restored and in the end God received all the glory. If you are like my friend and wondering why life isn't prospering, it maybe because you have connected to someone you have given your power to instead of the one who holds the ultimate power. Completely connect yourself to the Lord and He will take you places you have never been or could ever imagine.

"To be set free you must first break the chains that are keeping you from moving forward."

Keep It Moving

Satan is most successful in manipulating and corrupting the minds of lazy, unproductive people. Have you ever been sitting around at home, bored and out of nowhere a negative thought comes about? Mad that the thought even crossed your mind, you try to cover it up, but it won't seem to go away, like an annoying facial pimple. Now, we know that thoughts create actions and out of those actions spring forth our reality, whether good or bad. What I want share with you may come off as a bit, untrue, but no worries the scripture will be my cosigner. I was always quick to blame the enemy for doing bad things, or better yet, claiming God tempted me, causing me to fall into a sinful trap. In studying the word, I was speechless when I discovered that when we do things, it is because deep down inside of us we had a desire to do it. See the scripture says, "When tempted, no one should say, "God is tempting me." For God cannot be tempted by evil, nor does he tempt anyone; but each person is tempted when they are dragged away by their own evil desire and enticed. Then, after desire has conceived, it gives birth to sin; and sin, when it is full-grown, gives birth to death (James1:13-15 NIV).

Dang! There goes my excuse for many of the repeated

mistakes I've made. See being idol is the devil's fun zone, because you, yourself began thinking of things that potentially ended up manifesting itself into sin, giving the enemy something to thrive on. That is why as much as we can, we should seek to be productive and not laying around just waiting for life to happen. Try to stay productive, whether it's simply reading a book, writing, spending time with the kids, teaching yourself something new, taking a class, or finding things you're passionate about.

Cherish This Day

Don't worry about tomorrow for tomorrow will bring its own worries. Today's trouble is enough for today.
- Matthew 6:34 (NIV)

This is the day the day that the Lord has made, let us rejoice and be glad in it. Let us celebrate the existence of new beginnings, new hope, better understandings, a breath of fresh air, new strength, and another day journey with God. Live each day to the fullest, enjoying every glamorous detail laid out before our precious eyes. Today's hidden treasures are left undiscovered because we put off for tomorrow what should be done today. Stop worrying about days to come and embrace the joys of today's contributions. Fear not and do not be anxious about anything. The morning news can't save us, nor can worrying about job security, personal health, or the kids. Paul, in the book of Philippians, kindly tells us to worry about nothing, but in every situation pray about everything, and receive the peace of God. When your worrying seems to get the best of you and starts spiraling out of control try praying this simple prayer, "God, whatever the day brings, help me to focus on you. Guide me today and calm my worries. The Bible says, "Do not be anxious about anything, but in every situation, by prayer and petition, with thanksgiving, present your requests to God. And the peace of God, which transcends all understanding, will guard your hearts and your minds in Christ Jesus. (Philippians 4:6-7 NIV)

Loaded Baggage

See! The winter is past; the rains are over and gone.
- Songs of Solomon 2:11 (NIV)

Seriously! Why? I found myself balled up in a fetal position, with tears flooding the carpet of my closet floor numerous of times. You would think knowing better means nothing more than to do better, right? Perhaps not making the same mistakes and bad decisions is easier for you warriors who are taking this journeying with me, but for me, my baggage seemed to follow me literally everywhere, like white on rice. Every time I broke free from a negative experience, I found it yet difficult to mentally break free from its stronghold over me. The painful heartbreaks, failures, unaccomplished goals, abuse, and negligence from the past haunted my soul like a ruthless bully, who wouldn't stop until I was broken all again. So much so, that brokenness eventually became my familiar place. Every dream I wanted to accomplish, I quickly talked myself out of because a reflection of my failures boldly reappeared when I looked in the mirror. It took me six years to finish my Associates of Science Degree from a two year community college because the near thought of taking online classes in order to finish reminded me of the four failed history and government classes I could not seem to stay on top of. So instead of dumping this baggage, I went years believing that I was challenged when it came to taking classes online. I eventually allowed this baggage to postpone my studies, avoiding online courses at whatever cost. I allowed myself live in dysfunctional relationships, knowing that pain would result, but too afraid to say I deserved better. If the relationship was too perfect, I found ways to make it worse by expecting the worst, until eventually the worst manifested. Be careful of the things you speak over your life, for out of the tongue comes lies, life, or death.

My love, if you can relate in anyway, trust me, I understand. When you use your baggage for guidance in your present life, you are simply setting the stage and making it easier for sin to control you. After dumping the baggage, I was able to reclaim victory over my life. Not only finishing one degree but my Bachelors in Psychology in less than two years for the sake of overcoming my fear of online classes. Choosing to set higher standards and not torturing a good man with old baggage I was able to experience the love a princess, like me, deserved.

I encourage you to declare that your joy will no longer be snatched away so easily. No longer will you allow unnecessary baggage to weigh you down, robbing you from your future. Give it to God, and watch how quickly He throws it away. If it is not of Him, then it should certainly not be a part of you. The past is history; that is where needs to stay - in the past. God knows your every pain, every failure, mistake, and guess what? He still finds you worthy.

Throw
Out
The
Trash
Before

IT STINKS UP THE HOUSE!!!

REFLECTION

1). What are some things that you need to let go of?

_____
_____
_____
_____

2). What is keeping you from letting go?

_____
_____
_____
_____

3). How's your baggage affecting your life?

_____
_____
_____
_____

4). When will you begin letting Go?

_____
_____
_____
_____

Handle Your Business

Laziness brings on deep sleep, and the shiftless go hungry
- Proverbs 19:15 (NIV)

By the time you hear someone say these words, "Handle your business," you know that some type of action of some sort has to take place. I've seen some people use these words in negative scenarios, like right before an angry women go out and bust the windows out of her man's car because he was caught cheating on her. Perhaps, flattening all of his tires seeking revenge for breaking her fragile heart. On the flip side, I enjoyed hearing "Handle your business" when I was single mom trying to work a full-time job and maintain academic excellence as a full-time college student. However you perceive the term, use it as a way to motivate every fiber of who you are. Let's not sit around waiting for success to fall into our laps like some magical prophecy. No more procrastinating because actually doing something requires putting forth effort and sacrifice of convenience. Think about all of the time wasted on being satisfied or perhaps dissatisfied with doing just enough to get by. If you were to take a tiny portion of that time, maybe away from watching TV, or hanging out on social media and apply it to something more productive, I promise you would experience an elevation in your success and the reality of your life.

Don't wait until a tragedy strikes or something drastic occurs for you to get your life in order. Do it today because tomorrow isn't promised. God will bless you with the power to conquer unreachable heights, but He leaves it up to you to tap into your inner abilities. Think about it for a second. If God wanted to create pencils, furniture, paper, money, or clothing, don't you think He would have done so? Instead, He provided us with the resources like trees, cotton, and a brilliant mind to create these things for the world to love and desire. He didn't create one brilliant mind and stopped. No, you my friend have something extraordinary within you as well that the world is waiting to experience. Don't procrastinate as to why you can't go back to school, get a job, or do the things you are passionate about. Understand that you are powerful beyond measures, but you have to believe that you are. Speak over your life who you are and what business you plan to handle. Create daily affirmations and place them on sticky notes all over the house if you have to. Live by faith knowing that what you speak is already done. And as you take the first step, He will take the second and carry you through your journey.

"Handle your business" so you can enjoy the rewards from the fruits of your labor.

"Success comes to those who puts forth the effort"

REFLECTION

1). How are you handling your business right now?

_____

_____

_____

_____

2). What are some things that you keep putting off for later that can be done now?

_____

_____

_____

_____

3). What are your short-term goals?

_____

_____

_____

_____

4). What are your long-term goals?

_____

_____

_____

_____

5). How do you plan on reaching them?

_____

_____

_____

_____

What A Void

God sets the lonely in families, he leads forth the prisoners with singing; but the rebellious live in a sun-scorched land - Psalms 68:6 (NIV)

When you're broken, lonely, and hurting, it's not uncommon to look for ways to fill those voids in your life. The void consists of empty lonely feelings that stem from deep, busted holes in our heart and soul. Some of those holes are fresh wombs like a death of a loved one, a devastating break-up, lack of love and affection, or maybe an unexpected loss of what was once job security. Other holes in our hearts are old wombs, patched with large bandages, like childhood traumas, that never seemed to go away, no matter how old we get. Instead of turning to God to fill our inner most desires, we look to outside sources to satisfy what is missing, only to still feel incomplete. I, for one, am guilty of running to men, in hopes that they would satisfy my hunger for love. On this journey, I endured much pain until the light bulb finally came on and I realized that God is the only source who could truly fulfill what was a void in my life. Searching for love in all the wrong places, I had a lot of sex before marriage and was in and out of relationships, due to my feeling for love and completion that were missing in Neverland. I was always left feeling like a victim, who was used and abused. Never once did I stop to reevaluate why I was the common denominator in these painful experiences. Instead of taking accountability for my own actions, it was easier to play the victim card and simply blame men. But, tired of crying endlessly night after night, I turned to the only man who could satisfy my desire for love once and for all. It was time to nip this void in the bud. God didn't hide me from these painful experiences, but He healed me every time I was broken. I learned that a man could not completely satisfy my void, nor can a woman satisfy a man's void entirely. We can search in other people, what is missing in our own lives all day long, but true peace, strength, protection, and healing comes from our Heavenly Father alone.

If you are experiencing a void in your life that doesn't seem to go away, then before moving on to plan B, submit yourself to Christ and allow Him to fill that emptiness. I'm not saying that you will never experience any voids again, because I would be lying, but when you do, know that you are never alone because God is always present to comfort you. He's your healer, deliverer comforter, and active listener. Turn to Him, talk to Him, and let Him fill your void with something more permanent than a temporary fix.

Why The Poor Harvest?

> The harvest is past, the summer has ended, and we are not saved.
> - Jeremiah 8:20 (NIV)

My pastor couldn't say it any better when he shouts across the pulpit, "You keep doing what you've done and you're going to get what you got." That makes perfect sense to me when I think about the concept of this statement. Too often, we are set in our ways doing things that are unhealthy and forming habits that are shamefully addicting. No matter how hard we try to think positive thoughts about creating a better life, nothing seems to change. Searching exquisitely while trying to find unresolved answers as to why our lives are not going according to plan, we just end up nowhere. We even go to the extreme and selfishly blame other people for blocking our blessings. "If my wife or husband would've believed in me, I would be much further in life," or believing other lies like, "I'll never get approved for a business loan being a Black man, Black woman or a minority in America." Scrolling the pages of social media, we begin envying other people's success, looking to pick at their every flaw instead of celebrating with them. Galatians 6:7 says, "Do not be deceived: God cannot be mocked. A man reaps what he sows." God does not hesitate to bless those that are being a blessing to others. The same measure in which you are being a blessing is the same measure in which you will receive. I wish I could say that He didn't, but God knows our hearts and our inner most sacred thoughts. No good deeds, thoughts, or actions go unnoticed by Him. In order for us to harvest a fruitful harvest, we must restore the roots of our produce. What are you planting in this season so that you can harvest in the next season?

Remember, there are consequences for everything in life. Jeremiah 17:10 says, "I the LORD search the heart and examine the mind, to reward each person according to their conduct, according to what their deeds deserve."

Open Your Eyes

Jesus said, "If you were blind, you would not be guilty of sin; but now that you claim that you can see, your guilt remains."
- John 9:41 (NIV)

"What? Are we blind too?" Some of the Pharisees asked when they heard Jesus speak to the man who was once blind but had his sight given to him. After the Israelites were freed from Egypt, God hardened the heart of Pharaoh. Changing his mind after he let them free from captivity, he and his army charged after them. When the Israelites saw pharaoh and his army coming they began to panic and cry out to the lord. They began complaining to Moses, "Why did you bring us here to die in the wilderness? Weren't there enough graves for us in Egypt? What have you done to us? Why did you make us leave Egypt? Didn't we say leave us alone? Let us be slaves to the Egyptian. It will be better to be a slave in Egypt than a corpse in the wilderness!" But Moses told the people, "Don't be afraid. Stand still and watch the Lord rescue you today. The Egyptians you see today will never be seen again. The Lord himself will fight for you. Just stay calm." (Exodus 14:11-14 NIV)

Nothing has changed from their generation to ours. It would've been easier to fear and have doubt, if they didn't know the Lord. As people we spend much of our time fussing and complaining about things that are not going our way. We allow our adversaries to become our main concern, losing focus of God's blessings that has already taken place in our lives. Thinking we are in control, we become blind like the Pharisees, who asked if they were blind. God deliberately frees us from situations that were meant to take us out, so that we can give Him glory, but instead we find reasons to remain blind. Stop complaining! Open your eyes and realize all of the miraculous things that God does daily for you. In spite of your lack of gratitude, God is merciful and fights our battles because He loves us. The enemy comes to steal, kill, and destroy; but the Lord comes so that we may have life and have it more abundantly.

Taking Charge

"The mind of a sinful man is death, but the mind controlled by the spirit is life and peace."
- Romans 8:6 (NIV)

One teacher reminded me that being poor in the spirit is not always about being down in the mouth. "Ugh, poor old, pitiful me!" It's not even about wrapping up in rags and hand me downs heading towards the unemployment line for government assistance. Being poor in the spirit means to recognize that we are spiritually bankrupted before God. I remember growing up in a small country town, where it literally felt like I was trapped in the eighteenth century. Before leaving my small town, I turned to my favorite uncle for guidance, since my father lived so far away, and sweet Jesus, being a pregnant, confused, 19 year old was not easy. Instead of my uncle embracing my decision to have a child, his hurt for my decision came out in the most painful way that tainted my spirit for several years later. Cursing, he boldly said that my child wasn't going to be ish. I trust that you can use your own anointed imagination and figure out what word was actually used. He went on to say that I could never accomplish anything and that college for me was not an option because a child would ruin my chances of ever succeeding. When I looked to other people for advice, their insight was also slightly limited because of their perspectives of living but I knew what they thought was not God's plan for me. The advice I received from friends and neighbors, seemed impartially questionable, because I knew that God had promised me so much more, I just didn't know what that more was exactly.

No matter how harsh the journey would have to be for me to find my happy ending, I was ready to travel down that path. Instead of allowing other people's opinion to have power and control me, I took control over my own life. Every step you take, every decision you make, do it knowing that no other person has the power to dictate the outcome of your life. The journey isn't going to be easy, but the result of following your own hopes and dreams makes it all worth it.

Don't beat yourself down over what someone else says about you, for you are not created to please them, but to please God.

I encourage you to take charge of your life and know that whatever God has planned for you, no one can take that away from you. It is God's promise to you!

BE ENCOURAGED!

REFLECTION

1). What or who seems to have control over your life?

_____

_____

_____

_____

2). What can you do to take your life back?

_____

_____

_____

_____

3) When are you going to do it?

_____

_____

_____

_____

Perfection Isn't Logical

> We all stumble in many ways. If anyone is never at fault in what he says, he is a perfect man, able to keep his whole body in check.
> - James 3:2 (NIV)

While browsing through the kitchen décor at Target, trying to see how I was going to decorate my kitchen, my eyes ran across a towel that reads, "It's exhausting being this perfect! This reminded me so much of one of my favorite quotes from Charles Baxter that says, "When all the details fit in perfectly, something is probably wrong with the story." The mere thought of trying to do things perfectly makes my head spin recklessly and my stomach nauseous. I remember starting a children's literacy book club a few years ago, hoping to instill in the next generation something of value. Sharing this vision with supportive family members and parents of my daughter's friends, was exciting! I didn't hesitate at all, nor did I properly prepare, instead, I dived right in head first and went for it. Inspired Believers was our book club name, for the name itself reminded me of how believing in Christ should inspire us to live our lives full of greatness. However, making extraordinary decisions does not mean that mistakes would be eliminated. It seems I tried so hard to make things perfect and to turn what only started as a book club into a non-profit organization that I became exhausted in trying not to make errors. The funny thing about life that makes me laugh, is how life is full of ups, down, mistakes, and all kinds of unexpected setbacks we didn't see headed our way. When we see something we like or have our minds made up on the things we want to accomplish, we are filled with confidence that all will go as planned. But soon as unexpected mistakes happen, we become discouraged and mentally shut down our hearts desires to keep going and try it again. If we do try at it again, we put in a lack of effort in accomplishing it because the rearview mirror of our mistakes reminds us of the previous attempts and failures.

The apostle Paul wrote, "But he said to me, "My grace is sufficient for you, for my power is made perfect in weakness." Therefore I will boast all the more gladly about my weaknesses, so that Christ's power may rest on me. That is why, for Christ's sake, I delight in weaknesses, in insults, in hardships, in persecutions, in difficulties. For when I am weak, then I am strong" (2 Corinthians 12:9-10). Don't let perfection steal your joy. Look back, remember, but use your pains and mistakes as a redirection tool that instructs you on how to handle tough obstacles diffidently. God loves you just as you are, mistakes and all. Perfection is His job, not yours.

Sparkling Clean

The more the reality sat in on being a single mother, raising a beautiful baby girl, in a world so cold, gave birth to bitterness within me. Remember, I told you, this was not our plan. I thought for sure that God was planning to keep us together, especially when he intentionally told me to give up trying to do things my way, and move to Dallas, Texas once our child was born. The agreement was that I would move to a place more suitable to raise our child and that her father, my boyfriend, would come once we were established. Well, that wasn't the outcome, in fact reality was far from it. Ladies, I'm not telling you to doubt your man, but when someone tells you to go somewhere first, then he'll follow, please raise an eyebrow or two. I really feel that if he or she truly loves you, then they would be right there with you, every step of the way. Year after year, my heart grew cold as ice towards my child's father, because he didn't hold up his end of the bargain. As distance and state lines stood between us, so did lies, disappointments, and continuous let downs, one after another. By year four, my heart was as angry as an evil villain such as Cruella de Vil and the evil stepmom of Snow White.

What created such anger was when he called and with a frightened stutter announced that he was expecting another

94

baby, by another woman, when we still had unfinished business to tend to. Ewe! Messy huh? And so it happened! The last straw was drawn, bitterness consumed my soul, leaving me internally broken and angrily annoyed. Hatred towards my daughter's father over took me like a curse, I couldn't be shaken from. The simple hearing of his name caused excruciating nausea and resenting thoughts. I would do things to intentionally cause him pain and suffering, like used his daughter against him. Whenever he called her, I wouldn't pick up the phone and if I did answer I was too bitter to hold the phone up to my ear. Instead, the phone would lie powerlessly on the floor while I continued on about my day doing what I was already doing before he interrupted. As painful as this journey looks, I told you, hang in there it gets better. See, God has a funny way of working things out in the midst of promised victories that looks to be defeats. Have you ever heard the saying that God will answer a child's prayer faster than yours? I'm not sure how much faster a child's prayer is answered but I know through experience that he definitely hears the prayers of an innocent child.

My daughter and I always made it a nightly ritual to pray together before bedtime. Night after night for years we would pray together so much so that I knew exactly what she was going to say before she said anything. Trying to move from repetitious prayers, I told her she could pray and ask for anything and God would give those things to her. Suddenly, her four-year-old repetitive memorized prayers began to change. She began praying, "God please send my daddy to me, so we can be a family."

Every night she would ask, "God please send my daddy to live with us, so we can be a family."

The more my child prayed for her father, the more I felt God's presence working on me. It didn't happen instantly, but slowly, the poisonous bitterness seemed to dissipate to the point where my heart smiled at the calling of his name. Watching a four-year-old have so much faith, I began to trust God for my own wholeness. My prayer shifted to asking God to forgive me for treating my child's father with such unkindness. I wanted so badly to remove the bitter components of my character, but I knew it couldn't be done without seeking help from a higher power. Fervently praying, we both began sealing the deal with God. My bitterness for the way things turned out fled from my body. I was able to forgive her father, but most importantly he forgave me for the way I ruthlessly treated him. After being a single mother for five long years what looked to be a broken picture was pieced back together with the glue not made by man, but the glue of the Holy Spirit. We both knew it was God that brought us back together, allowing us to marry because he confirmed that when we were apart he was also praying for guidance and direction in his life. Ironically but purposely, it was the same time his daughter was praying for him to be in hers. Hebrews 12:15 says, "See to it that no one falls short of the grace of God and that no bitter root grows up to cause trouble and defile many."

Along this journey, I learned a valuable lesson. Life can get a bit messy causing you to take on sins and if not careful may defile you. But trust that God has the final say so. He has the power to can change you and create in you a clean heart. He can wash away any shame, regret, resentment, and bitterness, whatever has taken residence in you.

Let   Go   And   Let   God!

The One Who Invests

If there is a poor man among your brothers in any way of the towns of the land that the lord your God is giving you, do not be hardhearted or tightfisted toward your poor brother.
- Deuteronomy 15:7 (NIV)

There is a story told by Elizabeth Silance Ballard called "Three letters from Teddy," that warms my soul with joy, yet floods my face with tears every time I read it. It reminds me of how making a difference in the lives of other people does not require wealth or lack of it, fame or fortune, but simply a caring heart to serve others. This story is very detailed, yet empowering, but for the sake of our brief journey together I will summarize it as respectfully as possible.

There was a 5th grade teacher named Mrs. Thompson, who on her very first day of school told all of her students that she undoubtedly loved them all the same, despite knowing that was a lie. It was certainly a lie when sitting right in front of her was a student named Teddy, who she happened to dislike. I mean Mrs. Thompson seemed to dislike everything about Teddy, from the dirty clothes he wore to the stinky smelly stench of needing a bath lingering throughout the classroom. His hair was a hot mess and the fact that he didn't interact with anyone of the other children added to her list of annoying things about him. Mrs. Thompson sadly began taking delight in marking his papers with a big ole fat

F in red ink at the top of his work. But after reviewing Teddy's past records, Mrs. Thompson was surprised to discover that Teddy's previous teachers documented why the sudden change in his character had occurred. Teddy's first grade teacher wrote that he was a bright child who enjoyed laughing and was a joy to even be around. His second grade teacher wrote that Teddy was an excellent child also but that his mother was terminally ill and that his life at home wasn't so good. Teddy's third grade teacher wrote that his mother died and that his father didn't show him any interest in him at home. Lastly, Teddy's fourth grade teacher wrote, "Teddy is withdrawn and didn't show any interest in school."

Realizing why Teddy was so troubled Mrs. Thompson was ashamed at how she pre-judged him. The shame grew even more when all the children brought her nice Christmas gifts but Teddy brought her a gift wrapped in a brown paper grocery store bag. The kids all laughed at his gift when they noticed that inside the bag was a rhinestone bracelet with missing stones and a half empty bottle of perfume. To eliminate the laughter, Mrs. Thompson made known how she loved the bracelet and even put on some of the perfume. Teddy's words to Mrs. Thompson were "Today, you smelled just like my mom used to." When all the children left she burst out crying and that very day her heart was changed forever. She began working closely with Teddy and instead of writing him off as a looser or a failure she encouraged him instead. The more she invested into Teddy the more he began to lighten up to the world around him. At the end of the school year, Teddy was one of the smartest students in her class. Despite Mrs. Thompson's love for all the kids equally, Teddy became her favorite.

Teddy kept in touch with Mrs. Thompson letting her know that he finished high school, third in the class, finished college with honors, and went on to get his MD. Sealing the union with him and his true love, Teddy asked Mrs. Thompson if she would sit at the wedding in place of his beloved mother. She agreed and proudly attended wearing the rhinestone bracelet with the missing stones and the perfume given to her as a gift from Teddy. Teddy hugged and thanked Mrs. Thompson for believing in him, but with tears in her eyes she thanked him for teaching her that she too could make a difference. Three Letters from Teddy by Elizabeth Silance Ballard, Home Life (Magazine) © 1976.

What a beautiful story! Now, how might you chose to invest in someone else today?

REFLECTION

1). What are ways you invest into other people?

_____

_____

_____

_____

2). What have someone invested into your life?

_____

_____

_____

_____

3). How has their contributions to your life changed who you are?

_____

_____

_____

_____

Are You Open-Minded?

Jesus looked at them and said, "With man this is impossible, but with God all things are possible."
- Matthew 19:26 (NIV)

What do you do when your heart and spiritual mind are both locked compassionately to inheriting the blessing you know without a doubt belongs to you? Do you shut down your ability to believe when the journey towards receiving such blessing becomes a blur or do you allow your faith to carry you past your visual footsteps? Living in Texas for a few years, with consistent and steady income, it was time to upgrade from a two-bedroom apartment to our first home. Having a home was even more exciting knowing that my family would soon be reunited. I couldn't wait to have my own space where we could run, jump, and not feel like we had to tiptoe or walk on eggshells over our neighbor's heads underneath us. Finding a home that fit our budget, yet having the things we weren't willing to compromise on wasn't easy, but God showed us compassion. We fell in love with a beautiful home that met both of our standards and we couldn't have been more excited to close on it. Taking the advice from a well-known realtor, we decided to make a bid on this property through the U.S. Department of Housing and Urban Development or HUD. Our chances of winning this bid was thrown into a hat with many others while hoping that the luck of the draw fell on the bidder with the most favor. Taking no chances of losing this deal, my daughter and I prayed passionately with a picture of our new home displayed on the computer home screen, as if it was already ours. We began claiming and confirming in the midst of patiently waiting for it. At last the wait was over the realtor called, but it wasn't with the news we had anticipated. As soft as she could speak she whispered, "I'm sorry but I have bad news, there was one bid higher than yours."

Although I was saddened, I couldn't help but feel comforted knowing that God must've had something else in store for us. Wiping the dust from my knees, I continued on my search for our first home that God promised us. Three long months had passed but I had no luck on finding another home that could compare to what we had already claimed. Suddenly, a surprising call from our realtor that confirmed why God is so amazing despite what things may look like. With excitement in her voice, she said, "I have good news for you! The home you were hoping to close on is yours if you still want it!"

Confused, but excitedly I asked, "Wait! What happened?"

She explained, "The lady that bidded higher than you, got sick and wasn't able to close on the home, due to unforeseen medical expenses. So the home, went to the second highest bidder, which is you!"

Not only were we able to move into the home, but we were able to move in without putting a dime down. All the money we were saving as a down payment was no longer required. My love, be open to incredible possibilities. It's your winning season. Whatever God has for you, is for you.

Trash the idea of simplicity and open your minds to unreachable height.

Frosty Love

He has made everything beautiful in its time.
- Ecclesiastes 3:11 (NIV)

Oscar Bimpong once wrote, "Wishing is a form of inspiration for the lazy mind but taking action, persisting and finding alternative routes to your destination against all odds is the definition of a successful Venture." This quote resonates with my husband and I all so well. While planning to finally be united in Holy matrimony we couldn't wait to say," I do," and become Mr. and Mrs. Lewis but before getting there we had a ton of planning and preparation to do. We had to search for a venue to host the wedding ceremony, what colors to wear, the venue décor, who would be in the wedding, all the way down to the size and details of the wedding cake. Boy, was this planning experience stressful! I see why the TV show Bridezillas became so popular, I was a stressed out soon-to-be bride. Finally finding a beautiful venue to house the ceremony and the reception for 100 guests the pressure was eased to such a manageable memorable burden. It became even more at ease, when the venue was paid in full, hallelujah! I shouted to the rooftop as one of our major tasks was completed and there was finally light at the end of the tunnel. Invitations were mailed out with December 7, 2013 as the date to remember.

We were finally getting married! I couldn't help but rejoice at the thought of God bringing us back together and now uniting us in a covenant between the three of us. The previous five years of being without my prince charming made this moment so anxiously exciting! As the days began to wind down the report of the weather conditions seemed to not be in harmony with our harmonious plans. Praying that we picked a lucky day in December, the news reporter confirmed our luck had failed. Listening to the news all I heard was, "There's an arctic blast coming this weekend. We advise that no one travels out of town or on the dangerous roads if they don't have too. Roads are going to be Icey and too dangerous to drive on."

My heart fell to my toes and I cried out for hours in distress. Everything we worked so hard to plan was going to be ruined. The phone began to ring off the hook, family members all called saying they wouldn't be able to make the wedding. Friends texted to decline the engagement as if hearing my voice was a too hard to bear. My coworker who made our beautiful $400 wedding cake called and said she was trapped in her home due her inclined driveway was covered in ice. What really put the icing on our trapped cake, sending compulsive sadness through my veins, was hearing my mom and soon to mother-in-law say they wouldn't be able to attend the wedding either, due to the icey road conditions. The highways were blocked preventing them from traveling even if they desperately tried too. Seeing the heartache consuming me, my fiancé and prince charming said, "Stop crying, I love you. We're going to get married this Saturday, even if we have to face time the preacher." He went on to say, "I'm marrying you, not your family nor my family. God chose you as my wife."

Wow! Lifting myself up from my pity party, we went on to figure out a plan B. Before calling things off, God showed us he had a ram in the bush the same way He did for Abraham, when He was about to sacrifice His dear son Isaac on Mount Moriah in Jerusalem. Seeing that we couldn't travel safely to the wedding venue, we creatively turned my dad's home into a wedding venue overnight. Everyone who lived within a 30 mile radius from where we were hosting our wedding was able to attend. We didn't have to face time the preacher. No way! He happened to live in the same neighborhood as my dad so he was able to slide on in to marry us. Having favor all around us, my aunt's friend who happened to be a cake decorator at Sam's, created us a beautiful wedding cake, free of charge. My father put together an amazing menu, much better than the food choices we previously selected to feed the 100 anticipated guests at a 5 star venue. The ceremony took place in front of a beautiful, 10 feet tall Christmas tree with elegant décor glistening in the background behind us. Everything was so intimately beautiful, as God's presence filled the room. Reading our vows to one another, I was reminded of this quote written by Ikechukwa Izuakor, "Against all odds, when the "no" outweighs the "yes" faith becomes the only bridge to your answer."

I couldn't have asked for a more perfect wedding. It wasn't everything I could have imagined, no, it was so much more. Although the odds were stacked up against us, God was with us every step of the way. With our hearts filled with gratitude, we decided to throw my stepmom a birthday party at the paid venue, since we couldn't receive a refund. She was able to cater to 100 guests and our already paid for 3-tier vanilla, buttercream wedding cake was a gift to her as well. See, the enemy was trying to block our union by all means necessary but God had a way of using this storm for His glory. What the enemy meant for bad, God meant it for our good. Genesis 50:20 says, "You intended to harm me, but God intended it for good to accomplish what is now being done, the saving of many lives."

FIGHTING FOR LOVE

Staying True To You

For all the single ladies and men, looking to marry someday let me let you in on a little secret. See, I had the privilege of studying psychology during my four years of undergraduate studies and I discovered that physical attraction towards someone is so much bigger than the nice cars they drive, the figures in their bank account, or even the extended titles before or after their names. Don't get me wrong, these additives are great but what makes you more attractive to the opposite sex is being true to yourself. If your truth is being weird, meaning a nonconformist to who and what everyone else is doing, then by all means stand on your truth. If someone else has a problem with your uniqueness, then it's really their problem, not yours. The clothes you wear, the crazy hairstyles you rock and/or your optimistic views of this world are qualities that sets you apart from everyone else, thus making you more interesting to look at and talk to. I mean, if you were stuck on a subway with long hours awaiting you, would you care to be average and listen to the same old tired boring stories from someone you know or would you care to be enlightened by a complete welcoming stranger who has fascinating life stories to share?

I'll take the fascinating stories any day. My husband told me one of the reasons he is so attracted to me is because I am different from all the women he has ever dated. He loves the way I view the world and life's experiences. He certainly appreciates my confidence I have in who I am and not trying to be like anyone else. He has this saying, "My wife is one special person." I used to get mad when he said this because his meaning for special means that I'm a weirdo, very unique, and different but I began embracing being a special weirdo when I realized that this is who I am and he loves ever bit of it.

An original is far greater than a copy!

REFLECTION

1). In what ways are you unique?

_____

_____

_____

_____

2). What does others find most attractive about you?

_____

_____

_____

_____

3). What do you think stands out the most about you?

_____

_____

_____

_____

Neighboring Love

So in everything, do to others what you would have them do to you, for this sums up the Law and the Prophets.
- Matthew 7:12 (NIV)

Clinching our pocketbooks tightly coming out of gas station, "Sorry, I don't have any cash," we find easier to say than admitting we're tired of handing out money to around the clock shift beggars. All we're trying to do is go in the store, pay for some gas, and grab a snack for the ride home, that's it. But what if God turned His back on us when we needed Him most. As Jesus was leaving Jericho, a blind man named Bartimaeus was sitting by the side of the road begging. But when he heard it was Jesus, he shouted for Mercy. Jesus asked the blind man, "What do you want me to do for you?" The blind man said, "Rabbi. I want to see." Jesus then said, "Go, your faith has healed you." (Mark 10:46-52 NIV).

If you are having troubles understanding how to love your neighbors, I encourage you in your quite time to read Leviticus 19:9–18 and Matthew 22: 36-39, for they are great teachings about how to treat others.

Guard Your Power

And when God had me wander from my father's household, I said to her; This is how you can show your love to me; Everywhere we go, say to me, " He is my brother."
- Genesis 20:13 (NIV)

Do not seek revenge or bear a grudge against one of your people, but love your neighbor as yourself. I am the Lord.
- Leviticus 19:18 (NIV)

The foreigner residing among you must be treated as your native-born. Love them as yourself, for you were foreigners in Egypt. I am the LORD your God.
- Leviticus 19:34 (NIV)

Nourish Your Faith

> Don't let anyone look down on you because
> you are young, but set an example for the believers in
> speech, in conduct, in love, in faith and in purity.
> - 1 Timothy 4:12 (NIV)

Faith is the substance in which all things are made. It is the fairy to your pixie dust, manifesting all of your desired hopes and dreams. Consider your words to be the carriers of this pixie dust, as it has the power to be carried wherever you direct it. Through faith you can manifest anything into reality; good health, abundance, joy, peace, or whatever you desire. Our perceptions return to us, exactly what we see, meaning what we believe and hope for. Before I completed my first book, *"The Thrilling Chronicles of Mayfield,"* it was nothing more than but a bunch of broken memorable middle school stories, written down in a 99 cent composition notebook buried 2 feet deep beneath a pile of miscellaneous useless belongings in my trunk. I didn't see anything manifesting from it because I didn't believe that I had the capacity of ever becoming an author. It wasn't until late November 2013, my comfort zone of sitting inside a comforting cubicle, punching keys for eight hours a day was shaken up by a job layoff, and whelps, I was in that number. This job layoff couldn't have come at a worse time. than that. I was about to get married two weeks later and having a steady paycheck meant the world to me. Trying not to go bananas, I turned back to writing as my therapeutic escape from reality. I mean, I wrote about everything that crossed my 25-year-old cerebrum. I wrote every wedding idea under the sun, how I was feeling, what life would be like if I was rich, writing, hoping to stumble upon my purpose in life, you name it.

One evening while I was driving down the freeway, looking out at the curvaceous clouds and how they gently caressed the light blue skies within the clouds, God revealed to me a vision that forever changed my life. In the midst of the soft white puffs I saw in writing the words, 'Written by: Sharmetra Aubrey Lewis.' Every direction I took it was like this image was following me. Excited and hopeful, I knew exactly what that visual meant. I quickly ran home dug everything out of my filthy trunk until I found the fictional stories I had previously written about middle school. Not knowing when or what my next job would be, I didn't care! At this point I had mad crazy faith in publishing my very own book and becoming an author. Nothing else mattered, not how to start a book, who would publish it, nor what or how the format should be. I simply wrote and wrote with a sense of urgency and anticipation, while setting my eyes on the prize. People who knew me, thought I was a crazy loner because I pretty much isolated myself from everything. It was a criticism I was willing to take on because I was more willing to look ahead of what was next than on the circumstances in front of me. With the support from my husband, physically, mentally, emotionally and not to mention financially, I was able to complete and publish my very first middle school teen fiction, *"The Thrilling Chronicles of Mayfield."*

I shared this story to say that with faith all things are possible. Stepping out on Faith, with nothing but a cloudy visual, literally, and a heart for God, gave birth to a gift that I never knew was lying dormant within me, waiting to be discovered.

You may not see the actual road ahead of you, but know without a doubt that you are never traveling alone. Don't miss your opportunity to go for your hopes and dreams waiting to see all the details for our journey first. Faith requires that you move first. Your actions are God's trigger that you're ready to receive your blessings from Him. Like Noah building the Ark, real faith may require that you look like a fool for a little while but keep on building and dreaming anyhow. Step into your Destiny!

Unleash Your Inner Warrior

Hmmm, maybe I can do those things that other people believe I can do but I'd rather not try it. Instead, I'll do what's easier to handle to avoid going for it and failing miserably. If you're honest with yourself has these haunting words ever prevented you from reaching for the stars? Fear of reaching you instead settled for easily accessible pebbles on the ground. Come on be honest! Even animals have a way of settling beneath their calling by perfecting imperfections as a tradeoff. Do you remember the encouraging fable once told about the eagle who thought he was a chicken? When the eagle was very young he fell from the safety of his nest. Found by a chicken farmer the baby eagle was taken and raised amongst chickens in a chicken coop. Adapting to his environment, the eagle behaved like a chicken doing what the chickens did and believed what chickens believed. But, no matter how hard the eagle tried to be a chicken there was still something about him resembling that of an eagle. Trying to get the eagle to see his true potential he continued to struggle because looking at where he came from all he saw were chickens.

Finally, the naturalist who saw all along this eagles inner greatness spoke such powerful words to him, "Eagle, thou art an eagle. Thou dost belong to the sky and not to the earth. Stretch forth thy wings and fly."

Placing the eagle in on his arms and lifting him high into the sky the eagle stretched his large massive wings and took off above the skies.

Smiling from the depth of my core, I think back to when my daughter was afraid to step into her greatness also. Being in gymnastics since she was 5-years-old, flipping, jumping, and manipulating her body into weird looking ways was a piece of cake for her. But when it came down to learning how to do a backhand spring, she shivered in a panicked. Too afraid to trust her body with a safe landing she instead perfected back walkovers. Day after day, hours at a time, she disciplined herself to mastering back walkovers because they provided her the security of a safer landing. One day while watching her at practice I noticed that all the other girls in her class were just now learning how to do back walkovers. The coach believed in my daughter enough to go ahead and train her on a level beyond the rest of the class, but she was too fearful to embrace it. Knowing how courageous my daughter was I couldn't let her settle without at least trying it. At the end of practice, I asked the coach to wait a second. Walking over to my little gymnast, I bend down eye to eye and asked, "What's wrong? I know you can do this, stop holding back."

With fear in her eyes she whispered, "Momma, but I'm scared."

Comforting her I said, "If you do one backhand spring for me, I will take you to Sonic to get ice cream. I promise. No matter what, I believe in you."

With a smile big as the sun, she stepped back onto the mat, took a deep breath, and charged with a powerful run across the floor, completing her first backhand spring, with no assistance. Facing her fears, she kept doing backhand springs one after another. They were turning the lights off in the gym, but she was still doing backhand springs. High fiving the little gymnast in excitement the coach asked, "Wow! What took away your fears?"

Bouncing up and down she said, "My momma promised me ice cream."

When Destiny Calls

The purpose of a man's' heart are deep waters, but a man of understanding draws them out.
- Proverbs 20:5 (NIV)

Have you ever been pushed by a pain so heavy that it caused you to move towards your destiny? I'm not talking about the pain of stumping your toe on the bed rail, but those such as a job loss, heartbreak, financial crisis, health issues, troubled kids, marital problems, you name it. While the pain continues pushing you, making everything around you uncomfortable, God's vision starts pulling you, causing the pain to feel less forceful. But what happens now when God's vision is your number one priority and the only thing standing between you and your destiny is your faith? It's always easier to say, "Lord, I want to fulfill my purpose here on earth," but when He calls you to do so, you tuck away in fear like a turtle and hide. Our dear friend Peter demonstrates perfectly how we can lose faith in the midst of following God's calling on our lives. Jesus called Peter out of the boat and when he stepped out in faith and began to walk on water. Leaving his comfort zone behind wasn't too difficult to do, but staying the course was the challenge. Focusing on what things looked like around him, instead of focusing on Jesus, Peter began to sink. Having compassion, Jesus grabbed Peter by the hand, but was sure to acknowledge how little his faith was. The fact that the wind died down once Jesus took Peter by the hand lets me know that perhaps the storms we often face are temporary tests of our own faith. Peter could have experienced the miraculous joy of walking on water, like Jesus, but his faith limited his success.

You may not be optimistic like Peter and want to experience walking on water and maybe you have a burning desire to follow your dreams, but are hesitating to do so because of fear. Instead of following your destiny, you chose to adopt a life that everyone else is living only to discover that it does not quite fit well with who you are created to be. Whatever it is that God has for you, is for you. When destiny calls, don't be afraid to step out on faith and play full out. Don't wait on your friends, your spouse, or to get someone else's approval to begin your mission. Sadly, don't even expect for them to tag along on your journey or to care to hear about your progress along the way. What God has promised for you, only you can receive it. No man on earth has the power to control your destiny.

Guard Your Power

The man who plants and the man who waters have one purpose, and each will be rewarded according to his own labor.
- 1 Corinthians 3:8 (NIV)

And he made known to us the mystery of his will according to his good pleasure, which he purposed in Christ.
- Ephesians 1:9 (NIV)

In him we were also chosen, having been predestined according to the plan of him who works out everything in conformity with the purpose of his will.
- Ephesians 1:11 (NIV)

If a man cleanses himself from the latter, he will be an instrument for noble purposes, made holy, useful to the master and prepared to do any good work.
- 2 Timothy 2:21 (NIV)

Are You Dressed To Impress?

Finally, be strong in the Lord and in his mighty power.
Put on the full armor of God, so that you can take your
stand against the devil's schemes. For our struggle is not
against flesh and blood, but against the rulers, against
the authorities, against the powers of this dark world and
against the spiritual forces of evil in the heavenly realms.
Therefore put on the full armor of God, so that when the
day of evil comes, you may be able to stand your ground,
and after you have done everything, to stand. Stand firm
then, with the belt of truth buckled around your waist, with
the breastplate of righteousness in place, and with your
feet fitted with the readiness that comes from the gospel
of peace. In addition to all this, take up the shield of faith,
with which you can extinguish all the flaming arrows of the
evil one. Take the helmet of salvation and the sword of the
Spirit, which is the word of God.
- Ephesians 6:10- 18 (NIV)

Stand up for whatever your heart believe is right,
regardless of the consequences stacked against you. For
our Heavenly Father, He is a man of truth and righteousness.
Equality oftentimes comes with a price, a price I was willing
to pay for, when I was just a young lady, around 20 years
old to be exact. Taking on a job, as a local daycare teacher
wasn't my ideal dream job, but the benefit of receiving free
childcare I couldn't say no to that. Especially since I was a
young, single mother at the time, freshly new to Texas, with

125

no leads to any other jobs in the area. Bring it on hunny! Taking care of babies eight hours a day couldn't be that bad, so I thought. Whatttt was I thinking?! For crying out loud, both me and the babies, this job was as stressful as watching a ticking bomb getting ready to explode. I mean, everything was chaotic, from the organization of the leaders, to the disruptive, hyperactive toddlers, down to the ferocious dirty diapers that seemed to never stop tormenting me. Staff in higher positions felt the need to belittle those beneath them, not to mention the daily out of ratio child to teacher classrooms sizes, which really threw me overboard.

One day, being thrown into the lion's den with 10 precious quick on their toes little ones, I knew that I had all I could handle. Toddlers running around, others needing to be rocked and fed, what was I to do? Cast stones at me if you want, but I did the only true thing I could think of. Sliding my way into a ducked off corner in the room, adjacent to the changing table, I knelt down and called CPS, unanimously reporting everything. CPS came scurrying through the doors in a hurry, investigating everyone whose name was on the payroll. Now, word must've gotten around that I was the unanimous caller because my boss looked at me with dreadful fear when it was my turn to make known my truth. A sacred code as an employee, working in childcare, was to never tell the truth about inside circumstances, regardless of how wearisome they were but I was done simulating false truths. I was geared up and ready to stand firm with the full armor of God protecting me. Although my statements were confidential those who disagreed with my decision felt that I put the daycare in jeopardy.

Ooops! Unfortunately it wasn't enough to fire me, but reducing my hours to about 2 or 3 a day, making $7.50 an hour, was enough to officially call me unemployed and tapped out broke. Turning to God for comfort, He reminded me that you could never go wrong in His eyes, when truth is what you stand on. My love, I know it may seem problematic to stand alone in what's right but remember our God is righteous. Anyone who is not for Him is against Him. The truth will set you free from bondage, both internally and externally.

Take It Easy

"The end of a matter is better than its beginning, and patience is better than pride."
- Ecclesiastes 7:8 (NIV)

Relax! Take it easy! It's okay to slow it down a bit and not be in a hasty rush all of the time. As much as we like to think that time has the capacity to slow down just for us, it still ticks and tocks and we would be delusional to bet against it. But what we can be certain of, is that life is about maximizing every moment, both big and small. Yeah, it would be great to have the spouse, the house, the nice cars, and the college degrees with a nice lump of wealth set aside by the time we reach our middle ages, but all things happen in Gods timing. Try rushing destiny and you'll see that it never works out as planned. Instead it creates a whirling tsunami of impatience, confusing, anger, upsets, and broken relationships because instead of expressing gratitude for the right now, misery invades and takes over. I am so glad that God interceded on my behalf and slowed me down to a steadfast speed, which allowed me to capture ever moment around me.

Seeing the world from a steadier perspective makes my journey so beautiful and better to understand. If rushing for everything and not being patient for anything has been you, then I challenge you today to relax a bit. Take time to really enjoy every moment given to you, because once those precious moments are lost, they are lost forever. But if you capture them like a lightening bug, then you will always be able to store them in your memory and hold on to them for a lifetime. Patience, yet persistence is the key to living a joyous peaceful life!!!!!

Words Of Patience

A man's wisdom gives him patience; it is to his glory to overlook an offense.
- Proverbs 19:11 (NIV)

Through patience a ruler can be persuaded, and a gentle tongue can break a bone.
- Proverbs 25:15 (NIV)

But the fruit of the spirit is love, joy, peace, patience, kindness, goodness, faithfulness.
- Galatians 5:22 (NIV)

We do not want to be lazy, but to imitate those who through faith and patience inherit what has been promised.
- Hebrews 6:12 (NIV)

Bear in mind that our Lord's patience means Salvation, just as our dear brother Paul also wrote you with the wisdom that God gave him.
- 2 Peter 3:15 (NIV)

New Ways/New Ideas

"Get rid of the old yeast that you may be a new batch without yeast- as you really are. For Christ, our Passover lamb, has been sacrificed."
- 1 Corinthians 5:7 (NIV)

One, two, three, four, five, six, the count can continue until I get tired of counting. I'm counting all of the times I've tried to fit my old ways of living into my new walk with Christ. This was me, time and time again, "Yesss, hallelujah, I am not the woman I use to be!" Shouting, dancing and praising God in my little "CUTE" way, I thought this new path would be easy. Please notice the emphasis I placed on praising in my little "CUTE" way. Even though I was claiming to be born again, I was still more concerned about how I looked in the eyes of other people around me.

"Oooo, let me make sure I'm not shouting too loud, or let me hold back these tears so my mascara won't run down my face leaving dirty train tracks." I thought secretly. Or better yet, disturbing immature thoughts in the house of the Lord like, "Lord this message is gooooooooood, but I won't raise my hands to high because I don't really see anybody else doing it.

I thought that once I gave my heart to Christ and asked for forgiveness, from lord knows all the mess I have done, new ways and thoughts would automatically come. My spiritual bubble of automatic newness was popped right away because what I discovered was that accepting Christ is one thing, but changing my ways and getting rid of the old ones was another. Ladies, have you ever gotten a new purse that you were super excited to get? You took really great care of it, you wore it with every outfit in the closet, and was quick to show it off. But after a while, the initial high of cherishing it wore off and you found yourself treating this new purse just like all your old ones. You threw it around, sat on the dirty floors, crammed it with unnecessary junk, or better yet, it joined the party with the rest of your purses in La La Land, because, well, that's just your cycle of treatment towards your valuable purses. When you purchased this lovely, expensive, piece of material, you promised yourself you were going to take great care of it, and at first you did. But then you found yourself drifting back into the same old, tired out habits. Trust me, I know! I also know that old ways, habits, addictions, whatever it is that has always had a hold on you, has no place in the person you are trying to become. In order to grow in life, you must be willing to let go of that which has always crippled you. God wants to take you higher, but He can't elevate you if you are still holding on to the past. The person you once were is not the same person you are destined to become. Let Go and Let God.

Guard Your Truth

He is the rock, his works are perfect, and all his ways are just. A faithful God who does no wrong, upright and just is he.
- Deuteronomy 32:4 (NIV)

The Lord rewards every man for his righteousness and faithfulness. The Lord delivered you into my hands today, but I would not lay a hand onto the Lord's anointed.
- Samuel 26:23 (NIV)

May the Lord now show you kindness and faithfulness, and I too will show you the same favor because you have done this.
- 1 Samuel 15:20 (NIV)

He gave them these orders: "You must serve faithfully and wholeheartedly in the fear of the Lord.
- 2 Chronicles 19; 9 (NIV)

For the word of the Lord is right and true; he is faithful in all he does.
- Psalm 33:4 (NIV)

For the Lord loves the just and will not forsake his faithful ones. They will be protected forever, but the offspring of the wicked will be cut off.
- Psalm 18:25 (NIV)

Try Being Content

I am not saying this because I am in need, for I have
learned to be content wherever the circumstances.
- Philippians 4:11 (NIV)

I remember being anxious for things I didn't have,
that I overlooked the blessings right in front of me. Laying
in ICU, away from everyone and everything I loved, taught
me a valuable lesson, one in which will never be forgotten.
Blood sugar level reaching a deadly unbelievable high, close
to 1,200, made me a walking target for the death angel at
the age of 21. Being new to this selfish evil autoimmune
disease called diabetes was a pain. Like a thorn in my foot,
the agonizing pain would not seem to go away. It would've
been one thing to know my pancreas was lazy and produced
insulin when it wanted to but to selfishly stop producing
insulin all together, was just ruthless. There I laid, nothing but
me, the TV, an IV running from my neck, and a tan curtain
shielded across me, hiding my exposed pain and hideous
hospital gown. I wish I could say that I was grateful for still
being alive but at the time I couldn't because getting my
fingers poked every hour, seven days a week, non-stop just
drilled in my soul more sadness and pain. I couldn't escape.
I was lying helplessly in an uncomfortable hospital bed with a
Cather uncomfortably inserted into my sacred private space
devastated me.

I had no clue what I had done to deserve such pain. One of

my days in ICU, I was lifted from my self-pity and emptiness when a little girl, who was a part of a charity organization, entered my room and handed me a colorful handmade pillow covered in flowers and said, "Everything is going to be okay." This pillow today means more to me than any material, gold or silver. Finally, getting down to the bottom of things, with all of my test results completed, the doctor shared with me the news. He reported that I had what's called Diabetic Ketoacidosis, which occurs when the body produce high levels of blood acid called ketones in the bloodstream. On top of that bad news, he went on to explain that I was experiencing acute kidney failure and if I didn't get things under control, things could turn for the worst. For crying out loud, at that point, I was over diabetes! It was stealing my life away from me, right before my young eyes. Seeing my distress, he looked at me and said, "I know I shouldn't be sharing patients' confidential information, but the patient in the room right next to yours is battling the same complications. Sadly, her family have come to say their goodbyes because she's not going to make it. The difference between you and her is that you are younger, and physically stronger to fight this thing."

Realizing that God was sparing my life one more time, my whole attitude shifted. At that very moment, instead of falling into anymore despair giving the enemy more power over my life; I lifted my eyes to the Most High God. I am still a Type 1 diabetic to this day, but no more do I allow my circumstances to dictate my happiness. Correction, I have Type 1 diabetes, but diabetes is not who I am. I chose not to define myself by what I have or do not have, but by who I am and whose I am. To be content means to be in a state of peace happiness and satisfaction. It doesn't mean that life will always go as planned, but it means to learn to rejoice and celebrate all that God has already done for you.

Words Of Comfort

Even though I walk through the valley of the shadow of death, I will fear no evil, for you are with me; your rod and your staff, they comfort me.
- Psalm 23:4 (NIV)

You will increase my honor and comfort me once again.
- Psalm 71:21 (NIV)

When I was in distress, I sought the Lord; at night I stretched out untiring hands and my soul refused to be comforted.
- Psalm 77:2 (NIV)

Give me a sign of your goodness, that my enemies may see it and be put to shame, for you, O Lord, have helped me and comforted me.
- Psalm 86:17 (NIV)

My Comfort in my suffering is this: Your promise preserves my life.
- Psalm 119:50 (NIV)

As a mother comforts her child, so will I comfort you; and you will be comforted over Jerusalem.
- Isaiah 66:13 (NIV)

Shout for you, O heavens; rejoice, O earth; burst into song, O mountains; For the Lord comforts his people and will have compassion on his afflicted ones.
- Isiah 49:13 (NIV)

FIGHTING FOR THE KINGDOM

Hold Onto Your Dreams

"And afterward, I will pour out my Spirit on all people. Your sons and daughters will prophesy, your old men will dream dreams, your young men will see visions."
- Joel 2:28 (NIV)

Dreaming of a life beyond your current visual and physical horizon can be significantly enlightening, so much so, that it ignites the fire of your soul, giving it a reason to spring forward with an outwardly positive perspective on life, rather than a negative limited one. God uniquely gives each and every one of us dreams and visions to distinctly set us apart from having the same identity and destiny as someone else. Look at the world around us, the inventions, the creation of our economy, the way society operates and sustains in order to survive, or the way nature responses to our nurturing and non-nurturing characteristics, which contributes to each ecosystems survival. Your dreams, visions, and/or ideas are enough to make a life changing impact, whether large or small. See, God didn't make a mistake when he placed those thoughts in your mind and heart, which you have brushed off as, "Oh I don't know, something random."

Instead of exploring the possibilities, you quickly and secretly locked them away in a hidden compartment of your heart, waiting for more signs from the universe before pursuing them. No, these desiring visuals are God's way of revealing to us His purpose for our lives. PLEASE DON'T MISS THIS!

It's His way of speaking and communicating to us. If you're one who feels that God has never spoken to you, I'm no expert, but it could be that you're overlooking the messages, or perhaps you're closed minded to the channels in which He chooses to communicate through. But, what if that isn't you at all? What if you've finally came to a surrendering conclusion that you're going to trust God no matter what, as you pursue your dreams and ambitions, placed in your heart? You know who you are, and who you want to become, the sky is NOT the limit in your eyes, because to you, there's no limit. The only problem is, the more you set out to chase after your dreams, the more the road becomes foreign, lonely, and uncertain. What once seemed so precisely clear in your mind, now seems to be an obstacle course overwhelmed with challenging uncertainty. You're taking all the right steps with action but nothing seem to hint that you're almost there or fairly close.

"Come on God, at least a clue or two would be helpful and empowering," but nothing seems to budge, so you think. People are watching, both near and far, time is ticking, months and years are passing, money running low, and instead of seeing the work you've invested into reaching your dreams, all others point out are your setbacks, delays, and mishaps. This type of self-absorbed reflection have you doubting if it's even worth it to continue on, or if you should just give up because giving up is easier than sticking at it on your journey towards newness.

Before you decide to give up, I want to encourage you to hang in there despite the uncertainty or the lack of comforting pats on the back along the way. Trust me, I know the feeling all too well. That feeling of not knowing how I would get there or how long it would take me. For many years, I was the young woman who knew the desires God placed in my heart to seek after, but the way my life and bank account was set up (in my Kevin Hart's voice), had me awkwardly and uncomfortably stuck. Mentally, I was stuck because I couldn't see past what my physical eyes knew to be true. But as a believer in Christ, I challenged every part of my being to look outwardly with my spiritual eyes, knowing that with God all things were and are possible to those who believe. Spiritually I was able to slow things down enough to see God's divine presence and His gracious connections working things out for me.

Still to this day, I find that my flesh has me impatient with anxiety attacks that can only be calmed by the spirit within me. Whatever dreams you hold close in your heart, cherish them, nurture them, and be patient with them because God is indeed patient with you. Matthew 6:21 (NIV) says, "For where your treasure is, there your heart will be also."

Where Is Your Heart?

Fruitful Reading For Holding Onto Your Dreams

The Alchemist By: Paulo Coelho
Start with Why by: Simon Sinek

Find books you can read or audio to feed your soul daily.

"Be as careful of the books you read, as of the company you keep; for your habits and character will be as much influenced by the former as the latter."? Paxton Hood

Empty Your Pockets

> He who has been stealing must steal no longer,
> but must work, doing something useful with his own hands,
> that he may have something to share with those in need.
> - Ephesians 4:28 (NIV)

Ughh! I think I'm going to puke! I hate that every time I watch the news I see some poor innocent soul being slaughtered in the hands of heartless thieves. I mean if they wanted to possess the things they viciously killed to obtain why not work hard for them and earn it the right way? If it's not the news, then in childhood cartoon the theme of robbery is glorified. Robin Hood, as much as everyone loves to call him a hero, he still took from the rich and gave it to the poor. If they wanted the poor to have it, then I'm sure they would have given it to them without Robin Hood interceding on their behalves. Cranky as I may be, I can't overlook the fact that many of us have robbed from God also. You may be wondering, but how? Sure, I'm glad you asked. Through our tithes and offerings. I speak for myself when I say I'm guilty of cashing in my beautiful twice a month, sometimes three, paychecks to pay all the bills, hit the mall, and then scratching for chump change to throw in the offering plate, come Sunday morning.

Shamefully, still as an adult, I walk around with $5, $10, maybe even $1 dollar, just to look the part and not stick out like a sore thumb in the sanctuary. Sure enough, the same manner in which I gave to God was the same way He gave to me. It's hilarious, now that I've matured to know that God has a funny way of taking back what belongs to Him in the first place. Isn't it ironic that every time you shortchange God, things seem to break down at the wrong time, or a bill out of nowhere wipes you out, leaving you ashamed and broke. Why do that to yourself? God wants to pour down a blessing you won't have room enough to receive. All He asks is that we give Him our best of whatever that may be. I've learned to give it all up, my time, my creativity, my attention, my finances, or whatever can be given as a loving sacrifice. What are you holding on too, that's blocking you from overflow?

Receive The Benefit

For we died and were buried with Christ by baptism. And
just as Christ was raised from the dead by the glorious
power of the Father, now we also may live new lives.
- Romans 6:4 (NIV)

Delight yourself in the presence of God as you inherit the benefits of new life in Christ. You are no longer bound to the powers of sin, for you are no longer under law of sacrifice, but grace. You were delivered from such captivity when Christ died on the cross, in order that you may receive salvation. You were granted another chance at life, so now the choice is up to you. You can chose to live a life that you were promised or you can continue living in the flesh, controlled by sin. God is such a merciful and loving God that He looked beyond our faults and unselfishly made a decision to save us instead of giving up on us. Who would ever send forth their only son or daughter to die for a wicked nation that turned their backs on you?

I'm sure you're thinking hard about that answer, so it's a good thing God sent His only son to set us free. Wow! Ponder on that! That's some incredible love God has for us. My love, enjoy your new life, your new beginnings, putting all irrelevant things behind you.

NEW LIFE

Guard Your Power

Though we are slaves, our God has not deserted us in our bondage. He has shown us kindness in the sight of the Kings of Persia: He has granted us new life to rebuild the house of our God and repair its ruins, and he has given us a wall of protection in Judah and Jerusalem.
- Ezra 9:9 (NIV)

"Go, stand in the temple courts, he said, "and tell the people the full message of this new life."
- Acts 5:20 (NIV)

He has made us competent as ministers of a new covenant- not of the letter but of the spirit; for the letters kills, but the spirit gives life.
- 2 Corinthians 3:6(NIV)

So he went down and dipped himself in the Jordan seven times, as the man of God has told him, and his flesh was restored and became clean like that of a young boy.
- King 5:14 (NIV)

Longing For Money

Whoever loves money never has enough; whoever loves wealth is never satisfied with his income. This too is meaningless.
- Ecclesiastes 5:10 (NIV)

In case you may have noticed, I get a real kick out of adding a sense of humor to our journey together. There was a man who wanted so badly to figure out how to get more money that he asked a wealthy man could he borrow his book, How to Become a Millionaire.

"Sure," the wealthy man said.

"Thanks, but half the pages are missing," the desperate man made known.

"What's the matter?" the wealthy man asked. "Isn't half a million enough for you?"

As funny as that story is, I would probably be like the desperate man too, concerned about the other missing pages. Money, money, and more money was all I could think about. Heck, growing up without it, made the desire for it even more desirable. I remember envying people who had everything they could ever dream of and didn't have to lift a pinky for it. My goodness, every time I watched MTV Cribs and the Fabulous Life of whomever, jealously would rise up in me, like a rocket ship taking flight. Instead of celebrating their success, it made me reflect on the life I so badly wanted and the life I was currently living, which was not even close to being equal to one another. I was fed up with breaking my back, working extra overtime hours, to fulfill other people's dreams, only to barely have just enough to pay my rent, car note, insurance, and all other responsibilities.

Longing for the wrong answers to my problems, I began to acquire this attitude that I was willing to do whatever it took to become wealthy. I hooked up with a drug dealer with the intentions of joining in with his illegal business schemes of prospering, only to discover that his ways of prospering led him down an unfulfilling, unsatisfying, and detrimental path. His addiction to money became his slave master. The more money he made, the more he felt he needed and endangering his life for it, but didn't seem to matter. It was like having enough was not enough at all. Be careful what you long for because eventually it becomes your slave master.

Thank God for delivering me from such a crazy and dangerous relationship. As my attention shifted more to Christ, I began to be grateful for what I had instead of longing for what I didn't. No longer was I a slave to the desire for money because God showed me that He could bless the little that I had, if I put my trust in Him instead. Luke 16:10 says, "Whoever can be trusted with very little can also be trusted with much, and whoever is dishonest with very little will also be dishonest with much." The Bible also teaches us that, "No one can serve two masters. For you will hate one and love the other, you will be devoted to one and despise the other. You cannot serve both God and money." (Matthew 6:24)

DO NOT LET THE DESIRE OF THINGS AND MONEY DISTRACT YOU FROM THE GOD THAT BLESSES YOU WITH IT!!!!!!!!!

Balance Your Diet

A well balanced diet is the key to all happiness!!

Ugh! Same story, different day. My dietitian hammers me on eating right, every time I have a doctor's appointment. I literally sometimes plot on how I can slip out through the front door or jump out of a window to escape facing the reality that my diet is embarrassingly broken and uncontrollably unbalanced. Being a Type 1 Diabetic is one thing, but trying to balance life and my health can be a bit overwhelming. No matter how pretty I try to disguise my diet when explaining to my endocrinologist and dietician my blood glucose numbers, lab results are not ashamed to exposes all the lies. The sad thing about my denial is that dietary balance is mandatory but I forget that the balance is for my wellbeing and not theirs. I act like I am doing them a favor by eating crazy, then claiming I'm going to do better the next time around. I'm sure their wallets and pocketbooks are continuously fat, whether I eat right or not. That sounds like a reality check, when I say it like that huh?

Relating this balance to life, we all forget sometimes that without a balanced life, we cannot truly be prosperous as the stars in the sky. As one person, we tend to take on all the weight of the world, and we find ourselves overwhelmed, not by our strengths but our limitations. We'll work two or three jobs, go to school, raise the kids, cook and clean, run around like a chicken without a head, and do everything else that completes our daily routine of busyness. After doing all of this "BUSY STUFF", we forget to set time aside for God, so

He ends up missing in the completed equation. Or, maybe God is in the balanced diet, but only on Sundays and church better not last too long because I have a show and game to catch. Like food, we seek to eat daily for satisfaction, let's not forget the main course of the meal, our daily bread. Whatever your spiritual practice is, find time to devote yourself daily. Do this and watch the transformation that occurs in your life. Matthew 6:33 says, "But seek first his kingdom and his righteousness, and all these things will be given to you as well." Have you tried my God?

Power In Your Story

"Jesus did not let him, but said, "Go home to your own people and tell them how much the Lord has done for you, and how he has had mercy on you." - Mark 5:19 (NIV)

Your story matters! Yes, your story! The good, the bad, and the ugly. God uses your story to build bridges, mend broken hearts, and to reveal Himself through your journey. You may not believe this, but your story is the key that unlocks someone else's prison cell. The very thing that you were delivered from, someone else may still be going through. He's the only one who can turn your test into a testimony or your mess into a message. Why keep it to yourself? Your testimony is your chance to publicly and sacredly gives Christ both praise and honor. You were once a victim and felt hopeless in the face of your predator, but praise be to God for your victory! For years I complained, cried, and ran from my past hurts and pains. With an enormous amount of skeletons in my closet, I shamefully hid truths that only God and I knew He had delivered me from, with the fear of being criticized. Sealing those trials, burdens, failures, and broken pieces into a pirate's chest with an unbreakable lock, I buried my story deep within the depths of my soul. As much as I wanted to keep my story buried, it seemed that I was always placed in a situation that required me to release comfort to someone else, who happened to be going through a storm that God already brought me out of.

I find it to be a precious thing, when I'm able to help people who are not even close to being my age, both young and old. What was once too hard for me to handle became my antidote for healing in the lives of others. Look at God! Boy, does He have a way of working life out so that broken pieces suddenly fit into the puzzle of your life. I don't think there will be another Bible written that captures God's miracles that are happening right now in our present lifetime. With that being said, as a believer in Christ, it is very important that we share our stories with others. Not only are your stories meant to encourage other believers, but also the non- believers. Start sharing your story, right where you are. Don't wait until you feel you have reached the pentacle of success that makes you proud enough to boast about, but share it today. I starting writing this book as a young girl back in 2009, and we are now looking at me approach the finish line as an understanding woman in 2017. As much as I wanted to finish and have my name sealed as the proud author, God wasn't done molding and shaping my story.

My daughter loves to let it be known, "My mama writing a book she's been writing since 2009, can you believe that?" She really cracks me up and keep me on my toes. God isn't done with my story nor is He done with your story, but starting the process of sharing is so much better than waiting. Remember, the Lord sends a blessing through you and not just to you.

What are you waiting for?

Just A Little While Longer

So put to death, the sinful, earthly things lurking within you. Have nothing to do with sexual immortality, impurity, lust, and evil desires. Don't be greedy, for a greedy person is an idolater, worshipping the things of this world.
- Colossians 3:5 (NIV)

I'm betting my money on US! I truly believe we can hold on a little while longer and not submit to the ways of the world, regardless of how tempting things are. Oh Yes! You better believe it! I'm in this thing called righteousness with you. If God Himself, has that much faith in us all, why wouldn't I? The Bible says in 1 John 2:15-17, " Do not love the world or anything in the world. If anyone loves the world, love for the Father is not in them. For everything in the world—the lust of the flesh, the lust of the eyes, and the pride of life—comes not from the Father but from the world. The world and its desires pass away, but whoever does the will of God lives forever." As we make progress on stepping into the light, and staying in the light, let's keep our eyes opened for the traps that are out to inhibit us from entering the Kingdom. Don't think for one second that the enemy is messing with you because you are living wrong. No indeed! It's when you are trying to live a righteous life for Christ, that you are tempted the most. The temptations may come from the enemy, or they may come from our own sinful desires, but either way, we can overcome them.

We got this!

One trick I like to use when I find myself being dragged down by sinful thoughts and behaviors is I surround myself with people who are focused on positive things. I find people who have gone through what I am struggling with to mentor me. When I'm too weak to pray for myself, I find other strong believers to pray for me. Don't ever be afraid to allow God's people to pray on your behalf; however be careful not to let just anyone pray for you and over you. You don't want to mess around and have someone curse you into a stinky hairy mouse or a gigantic flying monkey do you? Relax, just kidding! What the Bible says about believers praying together in Matthew 18:20 is, "For where two or three gather in my name, there am I with them." James 5:16 also says, "Therefore confess your sins to each other and pray for each other so that you may be healed. The prayer of a righteous person is powerful and effective."

Keep your eyes focused on Jesus, and everything He has done for you. Let not His suffering go in vain, but honor Him with all your hearts, soul, discipline, and obedience. Hold on a little while longer!

TAKE NO PART IN WORTHLESS DEEDS OF EVIL AND DARKNESS; INSTEAD, EXPOSE THEM.
- Ephesians 5:11

REFLECTION

1). What are some things that tempt you?

_____

_____

_____

_____

2). In what ways do they affect your walk with Christ?

_____

_____

_____

_____

3). What can you do to help sustain from the sinful ways of the world?

_____

_____

_____

_____

4). What ways do you hope to benefit from holding out a little while longer?

_____

_____

_____

_____

Level Up

Because a great door for effective work has opened to me, and there are many who oppose me.
- 1 Corinthians 16:9 (NIV)

My daughter has me stuck on this show called Ultimate Beastmaster. This American competition reality show, on Netflix, has become one of our all-time favorites. It not only showcases American talents, but international talents as well as celebrities, TV stars, and athletes, as the hosts make it more interesting. Immediately introducing this to my peripheral vision, my interest was piqued, as my long lost competitive athletic nature began to flourish and awaken inside of me. My memory quickly jetted back to my high school basketball career when everyone called me a beast on the court. Not because I was ugly, stinky, hairy, or outright hideous, but because I was very strong with muscles popping out of my arms like some kind of trained bodybuilder. What I find intriguing about the competitors on Beastmaster is how well they train, year round, getting physically and mentally prepared for unknown challenges that await them. Each level within the competition has within it obstacles that are purposely setup to defeat the weakest links. The more levels one succeeds at accomplishing, the harder the obstacles become. Level one is usually easy, as long as the competitor stays mentally focused; he or she can get through it pretty swiftly. Boasting and feeling confidently ready for thw competition, some competitors underestimate the challenges that await them. Level two and three is when the pressure kicks in and causes the competitors to really dig deep within their hearts and soul to pull out all of the strategic strategies they've learned throughout their journeys, in order to overcome such faith testing obstacles. As you would probably guess, only the strong survives, and goes on to become Beastmaster champions. Those who completed the challenges were depleted after each obstacle course, because the difficult challenges took every ounce of strength and energy source within them to tackle such battle.

Now, comparing Beastmasters to life itself, the consequences of reaching new levels is the same. The higher you go in life, the harder the enemy tries to throw road blocks in the way to stop you. You'll find yourself wanting to give up and throw in the towel because the challenging difficulty of continuing on seems too hard to handle. It'll be times where you'll find yourself losing faith in God and in yourself, while wanting to turn back to doing nothing because doing nothing is easier. If you've ever heard, "New levels, new devils," then you certainly know there's truth to that disturbing statement. Don't ever think that you will reach a certain pivotal point in your life where you are free from challenges. No Honeybee, new levels bring new challenges. I like to look at new challenges as a clue that I've overcame a previous challenge and I'm now being elevated to face new ones. Like playing a video game filled with obstacles, I shout, "Checkmate along with thank you Jesus," when I succeed a difficult course. Don't be afraid to applaud yourself, you deserve that pat on the back. While the good seed you have planted is developing, don't fear or become afraid of a little weeds in the midst of it. In reading Matthew's 13:24- 30 (NIV), the parable of the weeds comforts my heart and soul, because it reminds me of how

God will use what was meant for evil to bless me.

I encourage you to mediate on this parable during your quiet time because it will truly enlighten you.

REFLECTION

1). Can you describe a situation in your life where there were weeds tied to your blessing?

_____
_____
_____
_____

2). What did you discover from that experience that has you viewing that experience in a more powerful and positive perspective?

_____
_____
_____
_____

3). Look at your life now, what has you feeling burdened down and do you only see more weeds than a harvest?

_____
_____
_____
_____

4). What do you hope to obtain from this harvest if you hang in there and not give up?

_____
_____
_____
_____

5). When are you ready to standup and face your obstacle courses? Why or why not?

_____

Count Your Blessings

Count your life as an overall blessing, not just the good things but all things. Pause for a moment, now, realize that where you are today is not where you were yesterday. Do you see the obstacles that God has delivered you from? Do you see that flaming, scorching fire that should've burned you, but instead it helped elevate you? Can you see that painful breakup as deliverance from something you thought you were too weak to release from? What about that job that laid you off? Can you see how God repositioned you into a place you would have never gone had you still been tied to that job security? Here's one more. What about that home you lost to foreclosure or to some bazar tragedy? With your spiritual eyes, can you see how God was showing you that He is your ultimate provider? Just when you thought you lost it all, He blessed you with a better home than the one you were torn to pieces over. See the journey wasn't so messy after all huh?

Out of our mess comes many blessings. God even loves us, in spite of us. He gives us chance after chance, when He could just said, "You know what, I'm sick and tired of this mess!" Be thankful for the life you live, for someone else is enduring far more pain that you could ever imagine. I shake my head when I think about how people envy my life, my marriage, and all of the blessings God has given us. People say the wildest things like, "I wish I had a marriage like yours or she think she's all that, because she wrote a book, and has a husband to help her." As much as I would like to say words that aren't holy enough to be recorded, I smile and think," If only they knew that with these blessings comes much burdens also." To whom much is given much is required. Being blessed doesn't magically wipe away pain and suffering. To want someone else's blessings means to also endure the pain and suffering that's tied to their blessing. The bible even says in 1 Peter 5:10, "And the God of all grace, who called you to his eternal glory in Christ, after you have suffered a little while, will himself restore you and make you strong, firm and steadfast."

As I traveled down some of the streets of South Dallas, Texas seeing those who are homeless, I have learned to be grateful for all things. From the smallest grain of salt to the home providing shelter for me and my family, count it all joy. And after you have counted all things in your life as a blessing, give thanks for being a blessing.

GOD
BLESS
YOU!

Live

You make known to me the path of life; you will fill me with joy in your presence, with eternal pleasures at your right hand.
- Psalm 16:11 (NIV)

Be honest with me, are you living or are you just surviving? Meditating on that question, I realized that I spent much of my life trying to stay afloat and not drown. Worried about how high the waves of the sea were, I robbed myself of being happy. Instead of fueling my conscious mind with faith, hope, and adventures, I loaded up my tank with fear, which kept my life parked in my own precious comfort zones. It was time I started living, fulfilling my inner most curiosities, and chasing after my destiny. No more would I wake up with the intentions of sticking to a daily routine, resembling the past 29 years of my life. It was time to set sail into a dimension overflowing with abundant everything. Abundant ideas, adventures, careers, passions, risks, whatever I dreamed of achieving. No more would I chose to be just a dreamer but a doer, with massive actions.

As we journey together, I want you to think about living and soaring too. You weren't created with a limited purpose to just labor for someone else and to pay bills all day, but to enjoy life. Start dreaming! Start planning! Start living! Plan yourself a nice vacation to some exotic place, write that book that's been in your heart to write, go back to school and get whatever degree you desire, tap into your passions, and live full out. No one has the power to dictate your reality but you. You only have one life to live, so live it up and enjoy every moment of it. My generation says, "TURN UP." God wants you to enjoy yourself, so turn down for what?

"Has anyone planted a vineyard and not begun to enjoy it? Let him go home, or he may die in battle and someone else will enjoy it." (Deuteronomy 20:6 NIV).

L.I.V.E.

Comforting Arms

"The Lord went ahead of them. He guided them during the day with a pillar of cloud, and he provided them light at night with a pillar of fire. And the Lord did not remove the pillar of cloud or the pillar of fire from its place in front of the people."
- Exodus 13:21-22 (NIV)

Trying to understand your place in this world can be a frustrating thing. It's one thing to know without a doubt that you are a child of God, but to know you are His child and not be clear on your purpose can be discouraging. You hear people say all the time, there is so much to life that exist far beyond what our eyes can see. The he say, she sayers are quick to say, "You can be anything you want to be and go anywhere you want to go, the sky is the limit."

I don't know about you, but trying to get there is always easier said than done. What's funny, is that the people who were encouraging you to stretch your faith and better yourself, are nowhere to be found when you need them the most. Who you thought were for you, are now whisperers about you. Turning their backs, they sit back watching with buttered popcorn and a soda pop to see how your journey turns out. With no one to turn to, not even a friend, you began second-guessing yourself, and wonder if you made the right decision to step out on faith. Oh, but tell the naysayers to take their time with their popcorn because there's comfort coming. Isaiah 40:31 says, "But those who hope in the Lord will renew their strength. They will soar on wings like eagles; they will run and not grow weary, they will walk and not be faint."

God has a way of sending the right people in your life at the right time, to help carry you into your destiny. Just when you thought you were limited by your own strengths and resources, God shows up in the mightiest way. I mean, resources and connections from those least expected amongst you will begin revealing itself to you. It makes me smile knowing that I can trust Him even in the midst of my uncertainties. The same way He guided the Israelites with a pillar of cloud by day and a pillar of fire by night, He will undoubtedly do the same for you. The journey you are destined to travel is led by God, so relax, don't worry about those who left you hanging along the way. To complete His mission, God will provide you with the right people, resources, and the knowledge you need to get there.

When God Smiles

When I smiled at them, they scarcely believed it;
the light of my face was precious to them.
- John 29:24 (NIV)

When God choses to send down His smile from the heaven, it comes at the most awkward moments; when you feel you don't have the strength to go on. At least that's how I see it. I want to share a sacred experience with you, which only a few have heard, due to the complexity of its understanding. As you listen with your spiritual ears, I hope that your soulful understanding is enlightened, as your knowledge of God elevates into a higher realm.

So, here we go. Being a Type 1 Diabetic has its perks, after all, who can deny me sweets when my blood sugar drops to a level demanding someone's attention. We call those the good lows, you know the ones where you only shake a little, temperature slightly rises causing you to sweat a little, and a little lightheadedness starts to occur. Slightly dropping below the normality of your familiar normal, this is nothing that a piece of candy or two can't fix. Popping in the candy or turning up half of a soda pop, whala, magic! Unfortunately there are those lows that happen in the middle of the night. These become a diabetic's worst nightmares because while we are comfortably chopping on some z's, we can possibly sleep through the early stages of warning signs. One night while I was sleeping like a baby, I started fading away as quick as a glow stick losing its radiant luminosity. Then it happened! Like a light switch being flipped on by someone in the house, my body began to communicate with me in the strangest way. Sounding like light energy flowing through an energy circuit, I could hear energy flowing through me. I could feel the particles circulating within my arms and legs, as if I was staring right at a circulation of protons and neutrons underneath a microscope. Bypassing the increased heart palpitation, extreme rise in temperature, and the disgusting pool of sweat, I noticed my soul rising inside of me like a balloon filled with helium trying to free itself. Instead of my soul leaving me, it was like it wanted to make itself known to me. I felt it circulating in a peaceful way that didn't frighten, but yet amazed me. It was there, in that present moment, that I discovered the separation between the physical body and my soul.

Lying there in dismay, I couldn't believe what I was experiencing. I mean, I always learned that we all have a soul but to feel the separation of the two was mind blowing. As much as I knew this experience was like none other, I knew I had to hurry and find some sugar, before I drifted into a Sleeping Beauty coma, awaiting true love's kiss. Rolling out of bed, trying to make it to the kitchen, my legs underneath me collapsed. It was as if I was as light as a feather, with no brain signal, telling my legs they were built for walking, or that my arms were created to lift things. "Oh boy, I thought to myself, this can't be good!" With all the strength inside of me, and knowing that my baby girl was in the nearby room asleep, I crawled to the kitchen in search for anything with sugar.

"Lord Help," I cried as I stretched open the refrigerator only to see the back walls looking back at me.

Making my way to the pantry, I found the one sure thing I knew would calm all this chaos down, SUGAR! Yes, I said it, sugar! Devouring a handful of sugar, like a plant needing water and sunlight, I prayed and trembled through the 15 minutes before I began to recover. Trying to find a balance, my body went from feeling like a 200 degree furnace to a freezing Popsicle outside in Alaska. The strength in my limbs was restored, and my soul no longer felt separate from my body. Shaking back to a stable condition, the soul's presence faded away from my conscious awareness. It only took one time for me to experience such a manifestation, to never want to experience it again, so I made sure I was fully prepared with a bedside snack. I've had several encounters with experiencing such internal power, and I must say, it is unbelievably incredible.

Some of you may have listened to this story and thought, "Oh my God, I'm so saddened she have to go through this!" But, I look at it and smile because I can see with my spiritual eyes God smiling back at me and showing me things that not everyone will ever get to see. Through the pain, He revealed Himself to me. I truly believed that gaining control of the soul's energy is where your true power is. And like the author Gary Zukav says, "True authentic power is when the personality comes to serve the soul."

So many of us are not aware that the soul makes separate choices and decisions from the flesh/ego, thus disempowering ourselves. I wouldn't take back these encounters with God for anything in the world. Had I not experienced such experiences, I would still be living my life only focused on the flesh, and not my soul, nor the spirit that's within. As you go about your own journey, pay attention to the details. God may smile and/or reveal things to you in the weirdest, most extreme, or calmest ways. Trust me, I know! And when that does happen, embrace it!

REFLECTION

1). In what ways have you experienced God's smile?

_____
_____
_____
_____

2). How was that experience to you?

_____
_____
_____
_____

Keep On Praying

> Keep on asking, and you will receive what you ask for.
> Keep on seeking, and you will find. Keep on knocking and
> the door will be opened to you.
> - Matthew 7:7 (NIV)

I'm so excited! We're almost at the end of our journey together. I encourage you to hang on in there to the end. Pray your way through distractions. You have the power to maintain and sustain. Whenever I find myself needing to strength from God, I turn to these few, but powerful prayers.

The Lord's Prayer in Matthew 6:9-13 (NIV):

"Our father in heaven, hallowed be your name. Your kingdom come, your will be done, on earth as it is in heaven. Give us today our daily bread, and forgive us for our debts, as we also have forgiven our debtors. And lead us not into temptation, but deliver us from the evil."

The Prayer of Jabez in 1 Chronicles 4:10 (NIV):

Jabez cried out to the God of Israel, "Oh that you would bless me and enlarge my territory! Let your hand be with me, and keep me from harm so that I will be free from pain." And God granted his request.

A Psalm of David in Psalm 23:1-6 (KJV):

The Lord is my shepherd, I shall not want. He maketh me to lie down in green pastures: he leadeth me beside the still waters. He restores my soul: he leadeth me in the path of righteousness for his name sake. Yea, though I walk through the valley of the shadow of death, I will fear no evil: for thou art with me; thy rod and thy staff shall comfort me. Thou preparest a table before me in the presence of mine enemies: thou anointest my head with oil; my cup runneth over. Surely, goodness and mercy shall follow me all the days of my life: and I will dwell in the house of the lord forever.

Surrender Yourself

But in their distress they turned to the Lord, the God of Israel, and sought him, and he was found by them.
- 2 Chronicles 15:4 (NIV)

I was a fool to ever think that I was in control of my own life. I spent years trying to do things my way. Having this egotistical attitude of "It's either my way or the highway." I thought that if anybody deserved to be happy, then it was me. Even as a young girl, I had this sneakiness about myself that did whatever it took to satisfy my own selfish desires, while disrespecting those who were responsible for guiding me. As if God didn't already know the cards in my hand, I thought I was the magical magician running the show. My goodness, what genetic strand did that confused apple fall from? Whatever tree this misunderstood apple fell from, I knew that I could not fulfill God's purpose over my life until I surrendered unto the Most High God. As promising as surrendering sounds, like a stubborn child it takes more than a promise to get us to submit.

Well, it did for me. This may not be you, but if it rubs you the wrong way, then you have my permission to say, 'Ouch!' I cried endless nights, feeling like a victim because my heart was broken from a relationship that God told me to get out of in the first place. But, because I thought I was Captain Save-A-Man, my heart was fractured leaving scars and bruise that never seemed to go away. I've gotten myself into so many fiery furnaces that God had to save me from or jump in with me to help keep my sanity. Like a drunk confused driver, I was about to cause my own deadly catastrophe. Like a poisonous snake, I was pushing venom into my own bloodstream, immobilizing my own ability to grow and prosper. The more I tried to run the show, the more the show ran me in a chaotic circle year after year. It was like hoping for different results but doing the same thing, the classic definition of INSANITY. If that's you and you're tired of doing the same thing, but getting nowhere, then surrender. Trust me, trying to do things your way will have you spinning your wheels in all the wrong directions, while delaying the promises. You may think He's waiting on you to get to a certain position in your life before He blesses you with this or that, but really God is just waiting on you to give up control. Rest assured that it's in His will to take care of you. The moment I let go of the steering wheel, was the moment that God began revealing Himself to me. It was the moment things began lining up for me and His words began flowing through me like a river of life. Words can't begin to explain how beautiful it is to be led by the Holy Spirit, dwelling within you. It's mind blowing! Simply Fabulous!

Sharmetra Aubrey Lewis

Life Story

Life
What a story
It has a beginning
A middle
An end.
The start
A lot may be fuzzy
Memories not completely clear.
We were cared for, loved and nurtured.
When we cried someone was always near.
The middle
Is compounded with memories
Joy, achievements, disappointment, laughter, and tears.
With twists and turns; perils from some decisions, temptations
to hard
To resist, to learn from:
To cry from
To hide from
To love from
To hurt from
The end?
We want know until it's time to cross over to the other side;
that
Closing statement to tell of what we're made.
When the last word is written, the last page is turned.
Our life's story would have come to an end.
Lord, before I close my eyes and take my last breath,
Allow me one moment to review the chapters that I've lived.
I pray there will be a smile on my face for most of the choices

that I'd
Made, and feel content to say The End.
Cover me Lord with your amazing grace.
The End
Aleelee (one who weeps)

Words From Your Soul To The Ego

Written by: Sharmetra Aubrey Lewis

Listen to your soul you stubborn Ego
You, me, and God, we're the perfect Trio
Don't you see that I'm pleading and begging to be free?
You pray for courage and faith small as a mustard seed.
When opportunities call for you, you tuck your head and hide
Like a turtle, buried inside, you stand behind your pride.
Why do you hold me captive to a life beneath my calling?
I want to soar high like an eagle, not like the birds that's falling.
You and I can work wonders together and wither any storm
Travel the world, live freely, if only you shared the platform.
I'm here for a purpose and that purpose is to unselfishly guide you
Open your eyes to new adventures, but you act like I'm the flu.
From the soul to your ego, I ask that you believe
Remove the pillow, so I can breathe and together we can succeed…

Why Wait

Written by: Sharmetra Aubrey Lewis

Why are you still standing there?
Whose permission are you waiting on?
Wasn't it you who cried out loud, about your dreams being on hold too long?
Those same dreams that excite you
Turn around and frightens you
Until you dream no more
The fear inside is preparing your mind to walk through an unknown door
Your dreams require actions, with a little bit of passion, to transport you like a car
Do it now, so that you don't look back and be left with an ugly scar

About The Author

 Sharmetra Aubrey Lewis, is an author, inspirational speaker, and youth mentor, who focuses on helping others discover their inner potential through writing techniques and encouraging support. Utilizing personal experiences tied with biblical principles, Sharmetra inspires both women and children to not be afraid of who they are nor what they've gone through, but yet embrace their stories as God's gift of light unto the world. She is the author of "The Thrilling Chronicles of Mayfield."

Sharmetra Aubrey Lewis
lewisssharmetra@gmail.com
214-543-7493

If somehow this book made its way to you, then my sister or brother this is for you. My prayer is that you find assurance in my journey, knowing that even in the midst of your own troubles, God always gets the Glory. I'm sharing my journey to remind you that whatever pain you go through, God will use to bless others through you. Stand firm and be encouraged.

Sharmetra Aubrey Lewis

Made in the USA
Middletown, DE
01 December 2021